DON BOUSQUET

REVENGE OF THE QUAHOG

HAZARD TO NAVIGATION IV
DON BOUSQUET

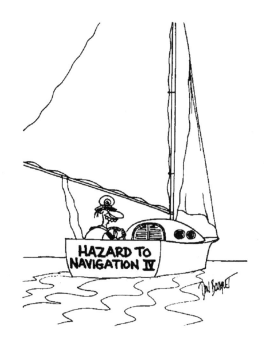

Covered Bridge Press
North Attleborough, Massachusetts

laughter and love makes it happen
Love
Brenda
9-99

Covered Bridge Press
7 Adamsdale Road
N. Attleborough, MA 02760
(508) 761-7721

Printed in the United States of America

First Edition

ISBN 1-58066-020-7

10 9 8 7 6 5 4 3 2 1

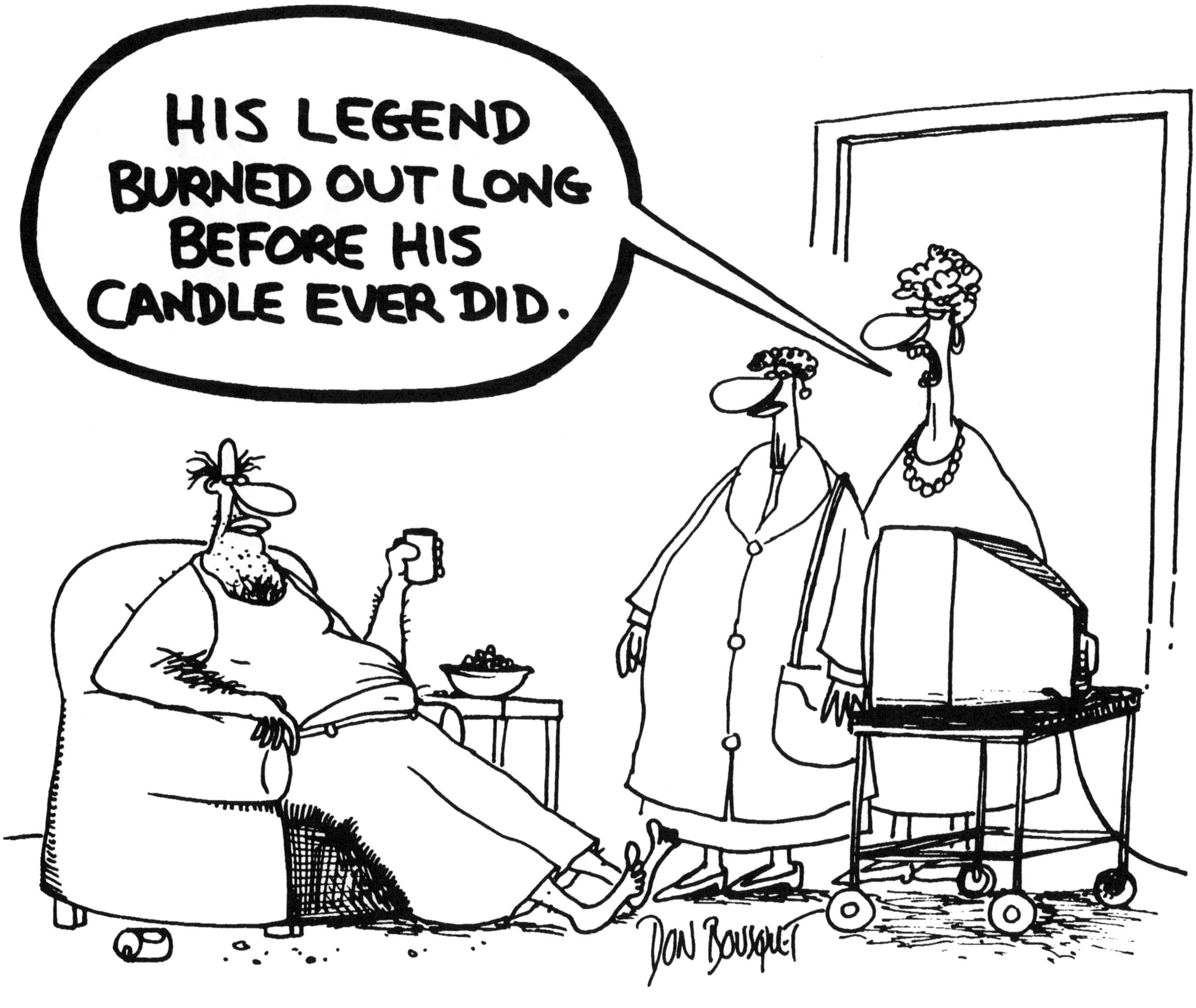
HIS LEGEND BURNED OUT LONG BEFORE HIS CANDLE EVER DID.
DON BOUSQUET

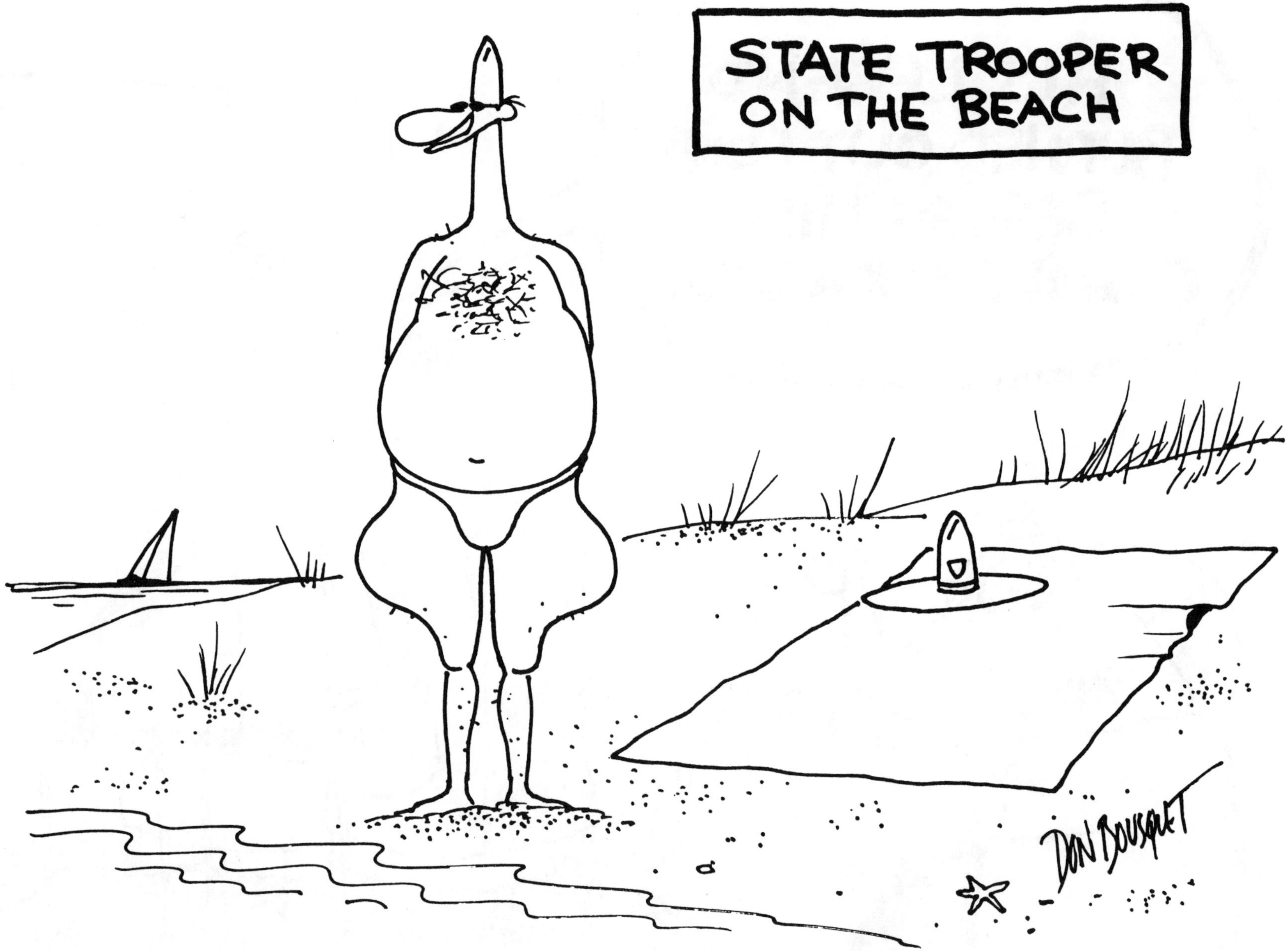
STATE TROOPER
ON THE BEACH
DON BOUSQUET

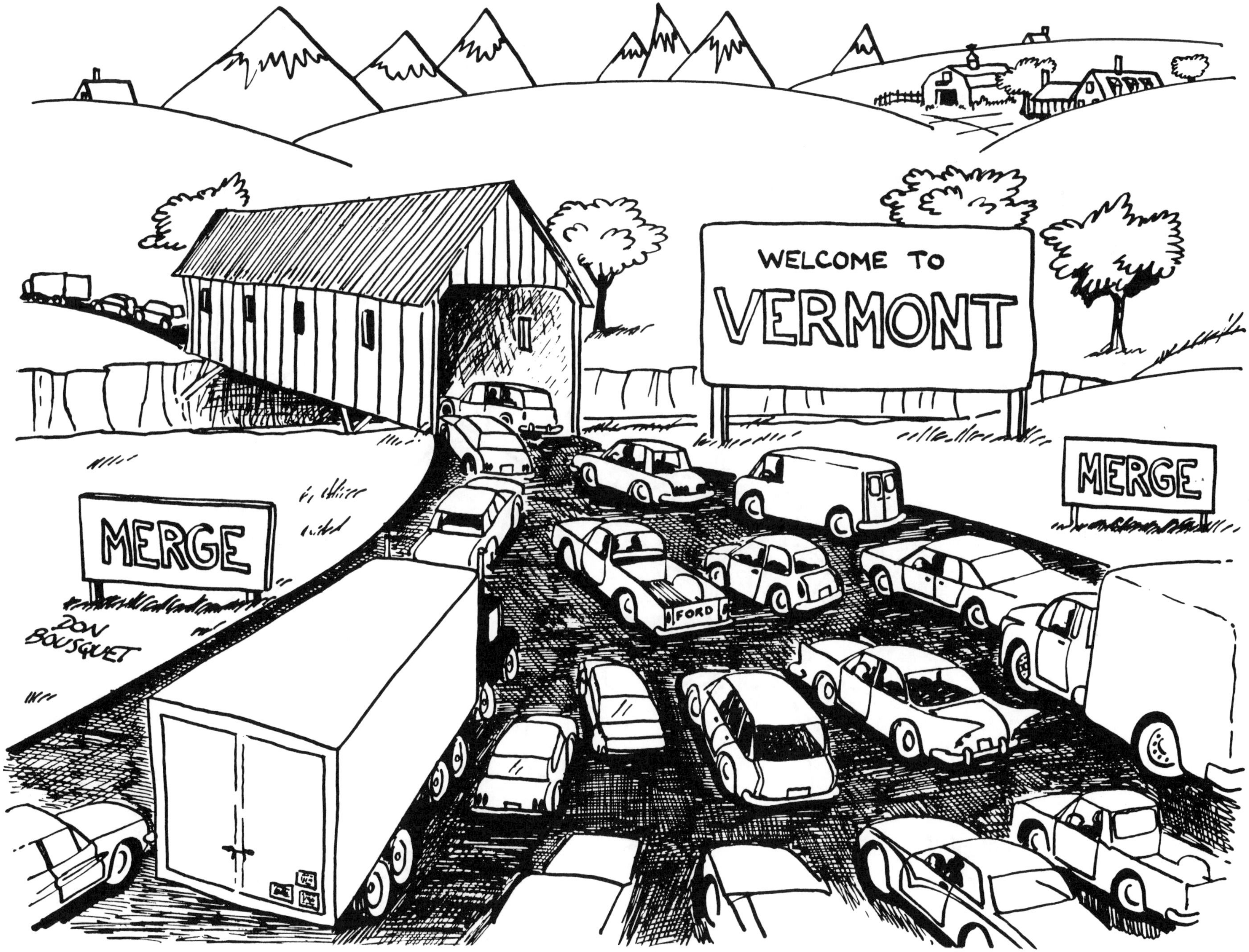
WELCOME TO
VERMONT
MERGE
MERGE
FORD
DON BOUSQUET

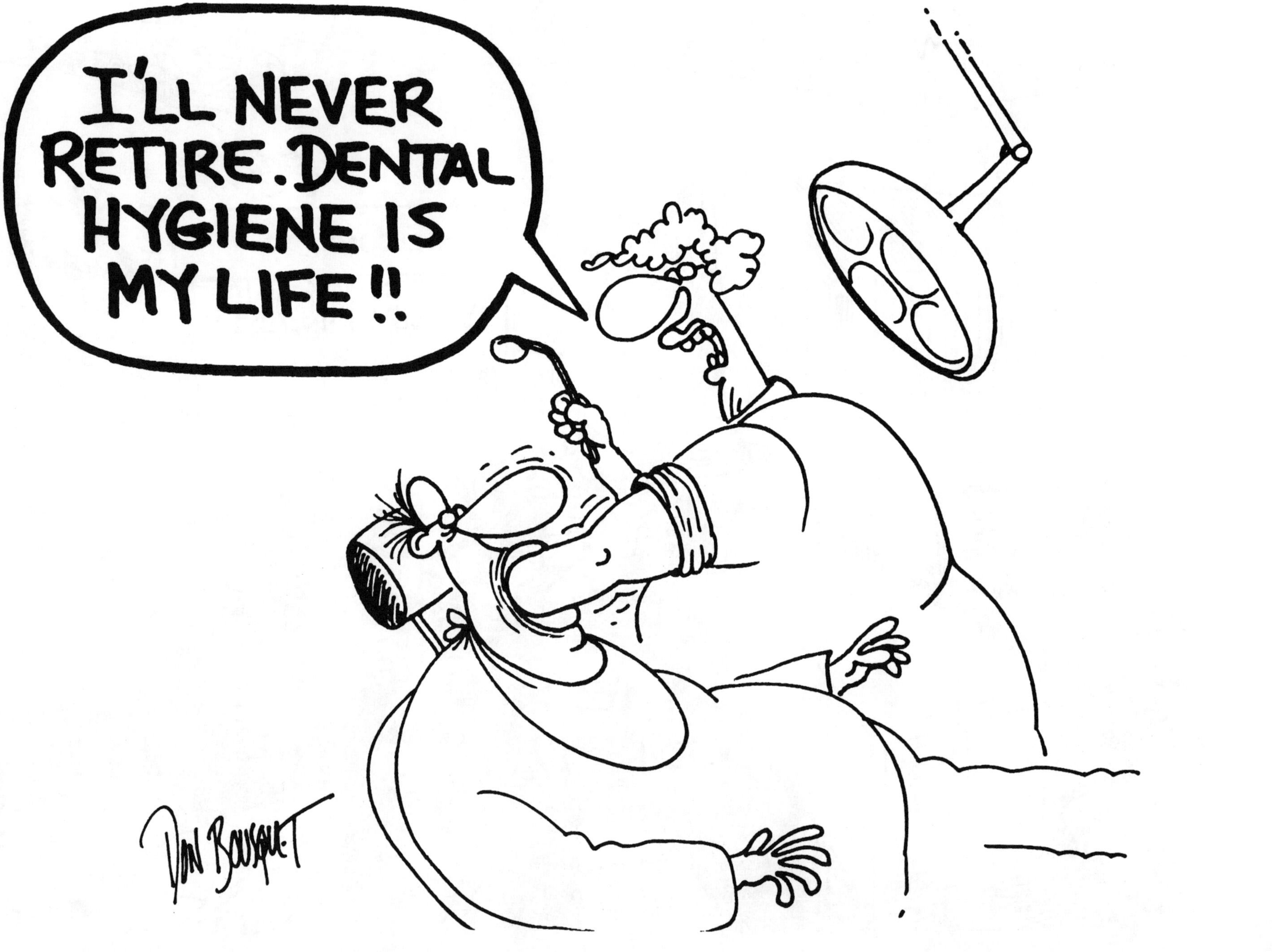
I'LL NEVER RETIRE. DENTAL HYGIENE IS MY LIFE!!
DON BOUSQUET

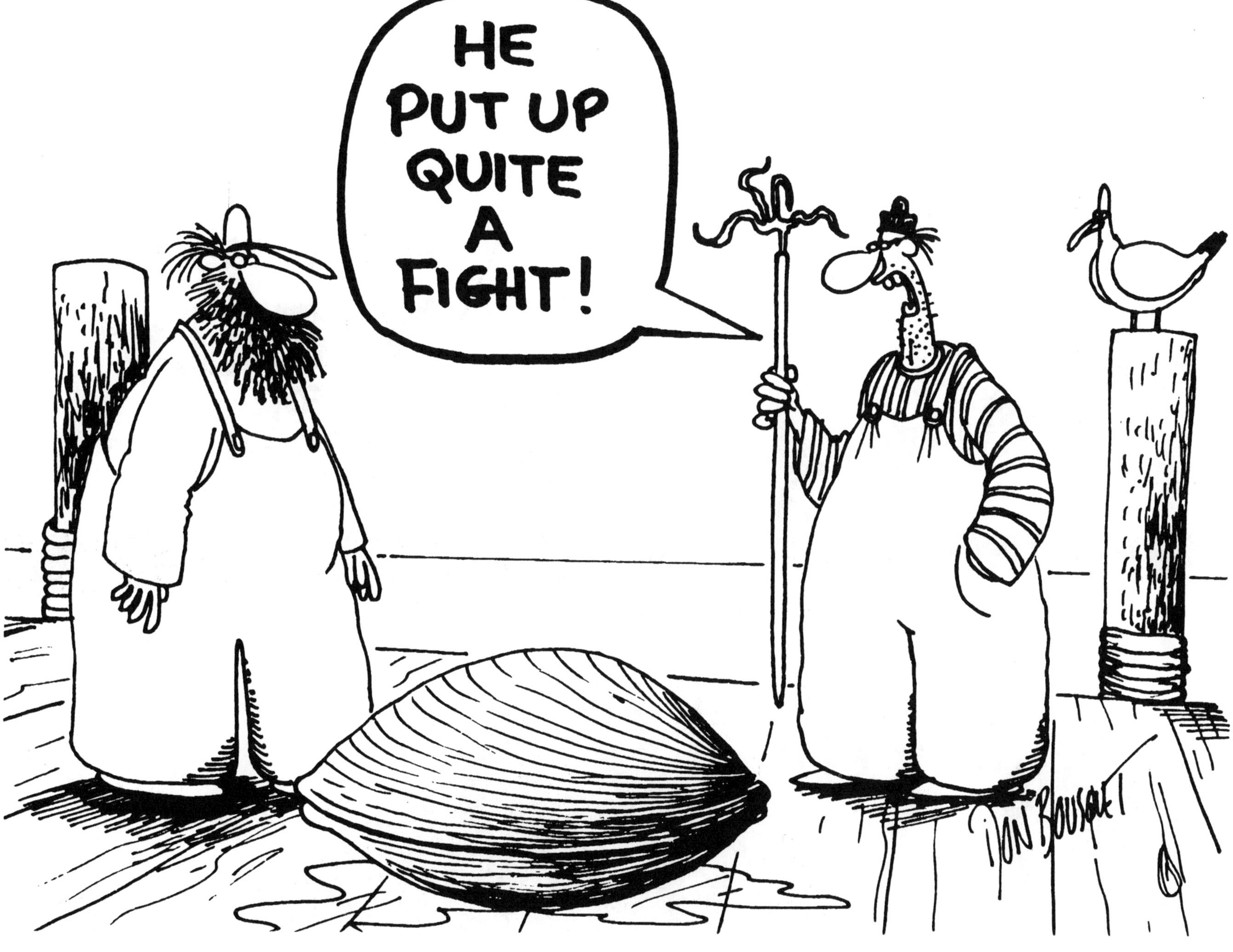
HE PUT UP QUITE A FIGHT!
DON BOUSQUET

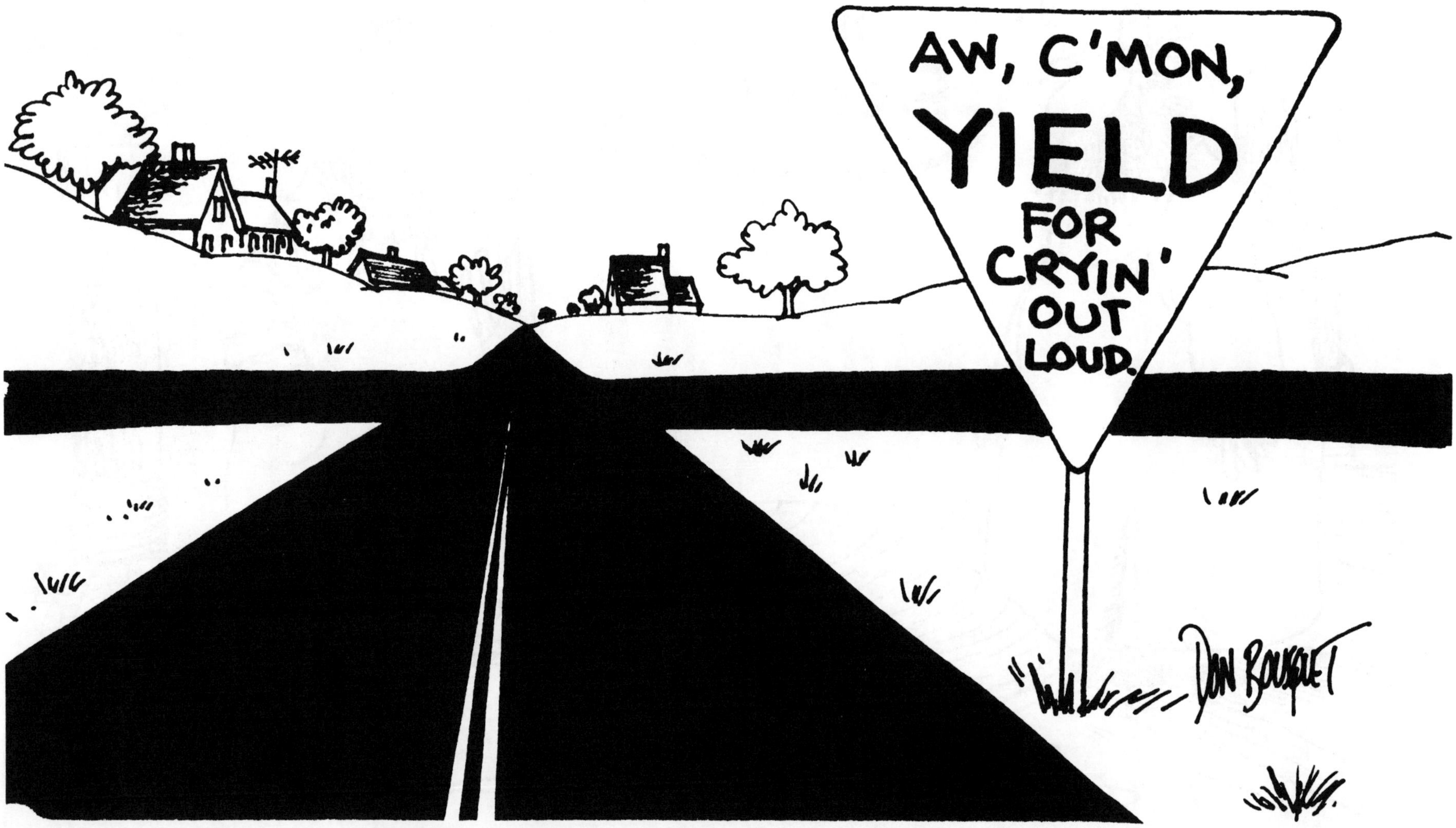
AW, C'MON,
YIELD
FOR
CRYIN'
OUT
LOUD.
DON BOUSQUET

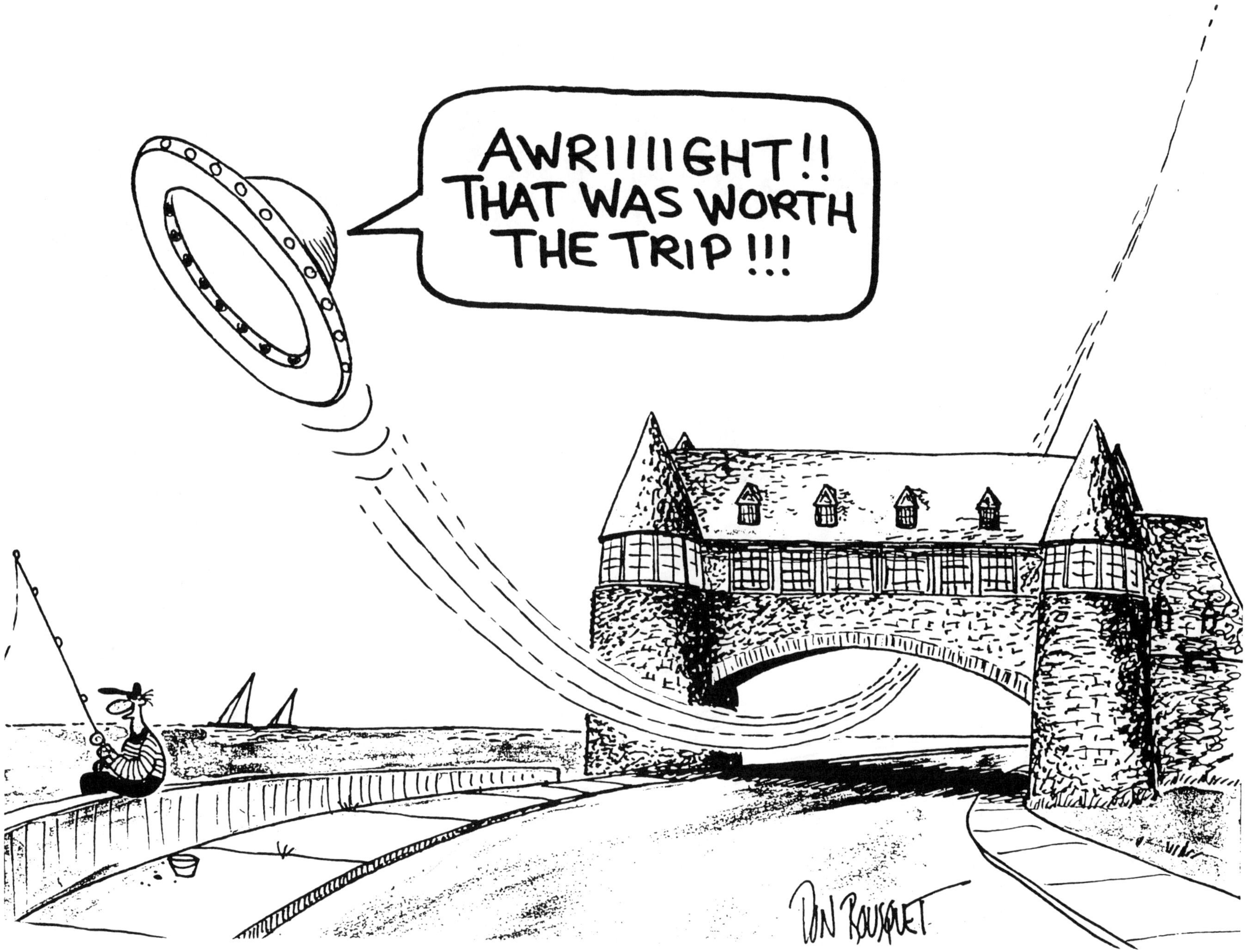
AWRIIIIGHT!! THAT WAS WORTH THE TRIP!!!
DON BOUSQUET

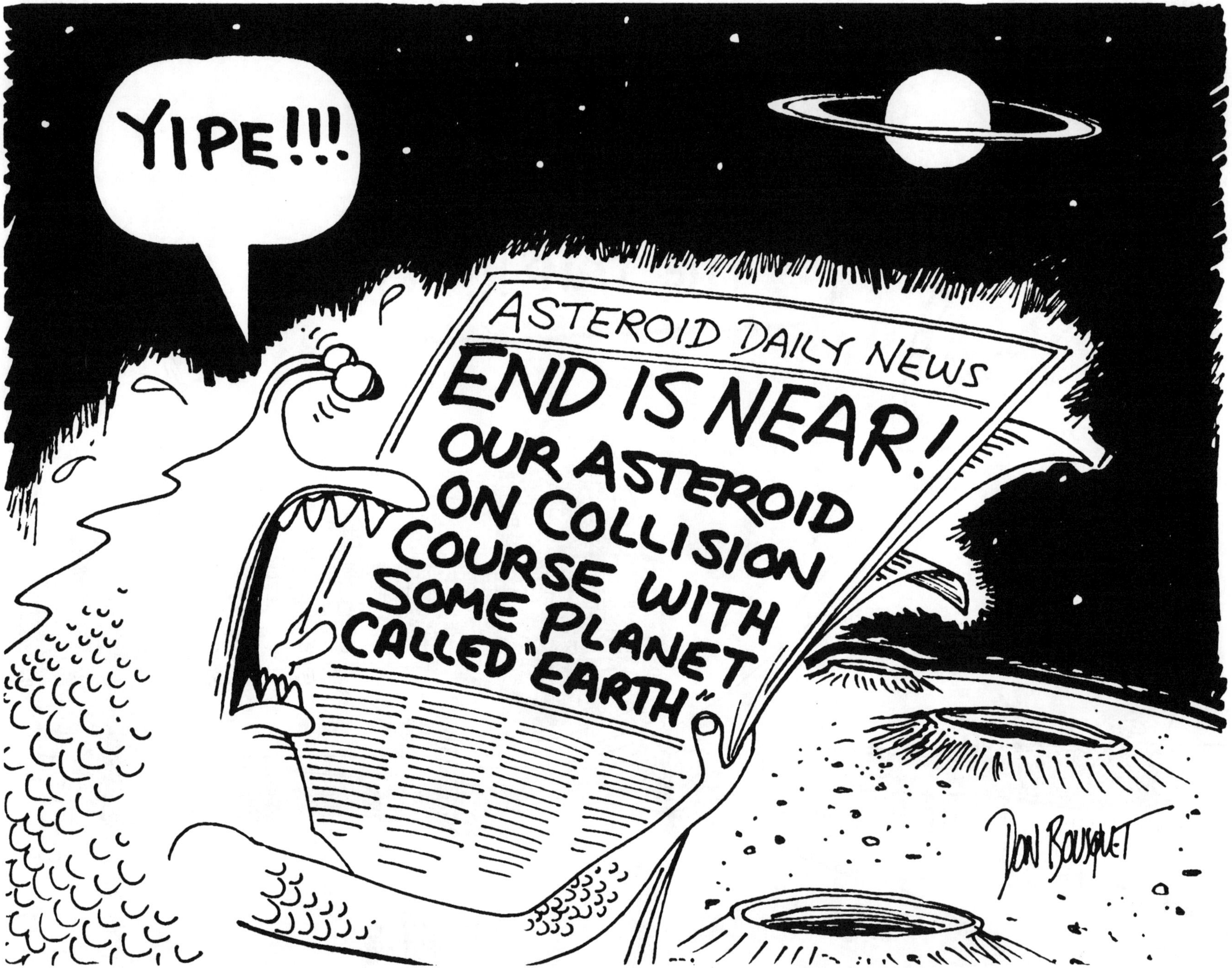
YIPE!!!
ASTEROID DAILY NEWS
END IS NEAR!
OUR ASTEROID ON COLLISION COURSE WITH SOME PLANET CALLED "EARTH"
DON BOUSQUET

GIANT BLUEFIN QUAHOGS CAN ONLY BE TAKEN LEGALLY WITH BOW AND ARROW.

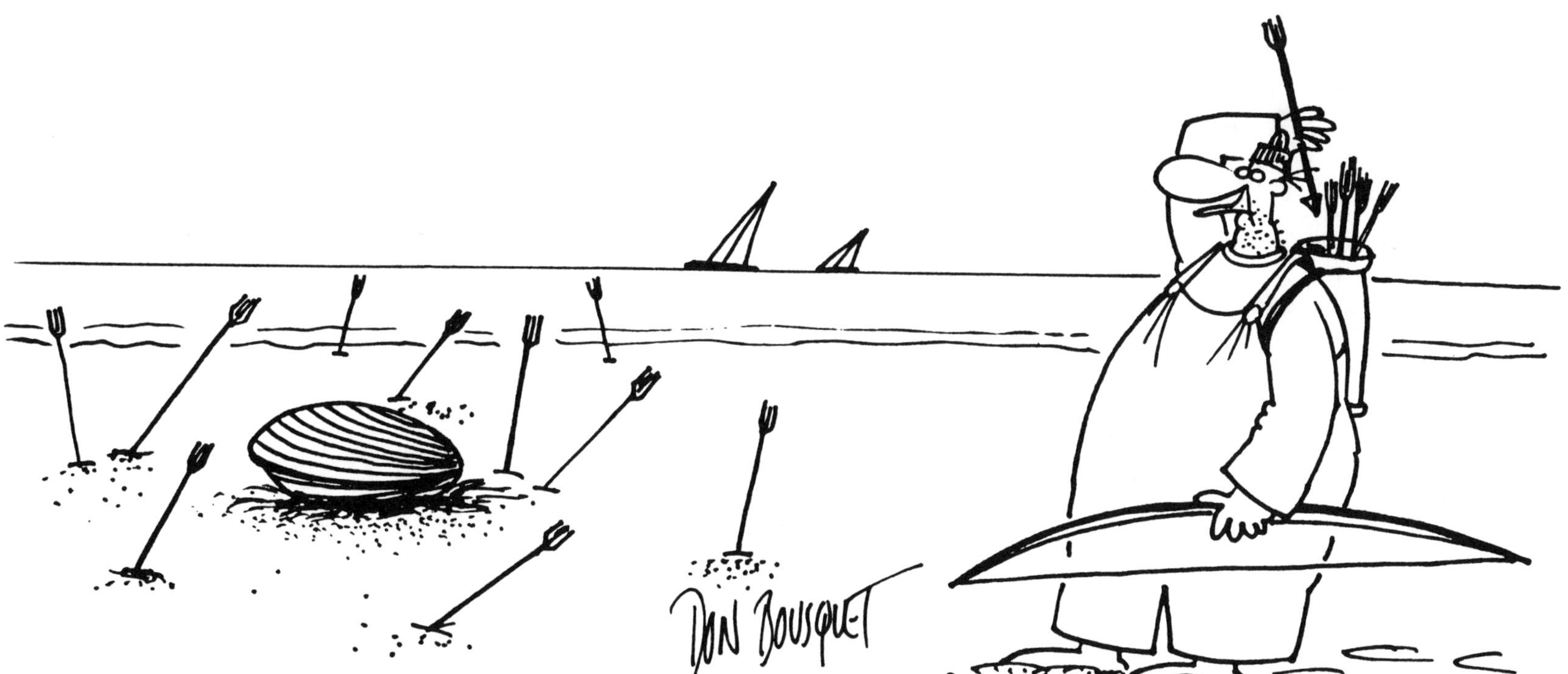
DON BOUSQUET

ANOTHER ONE WASHED ASHORE

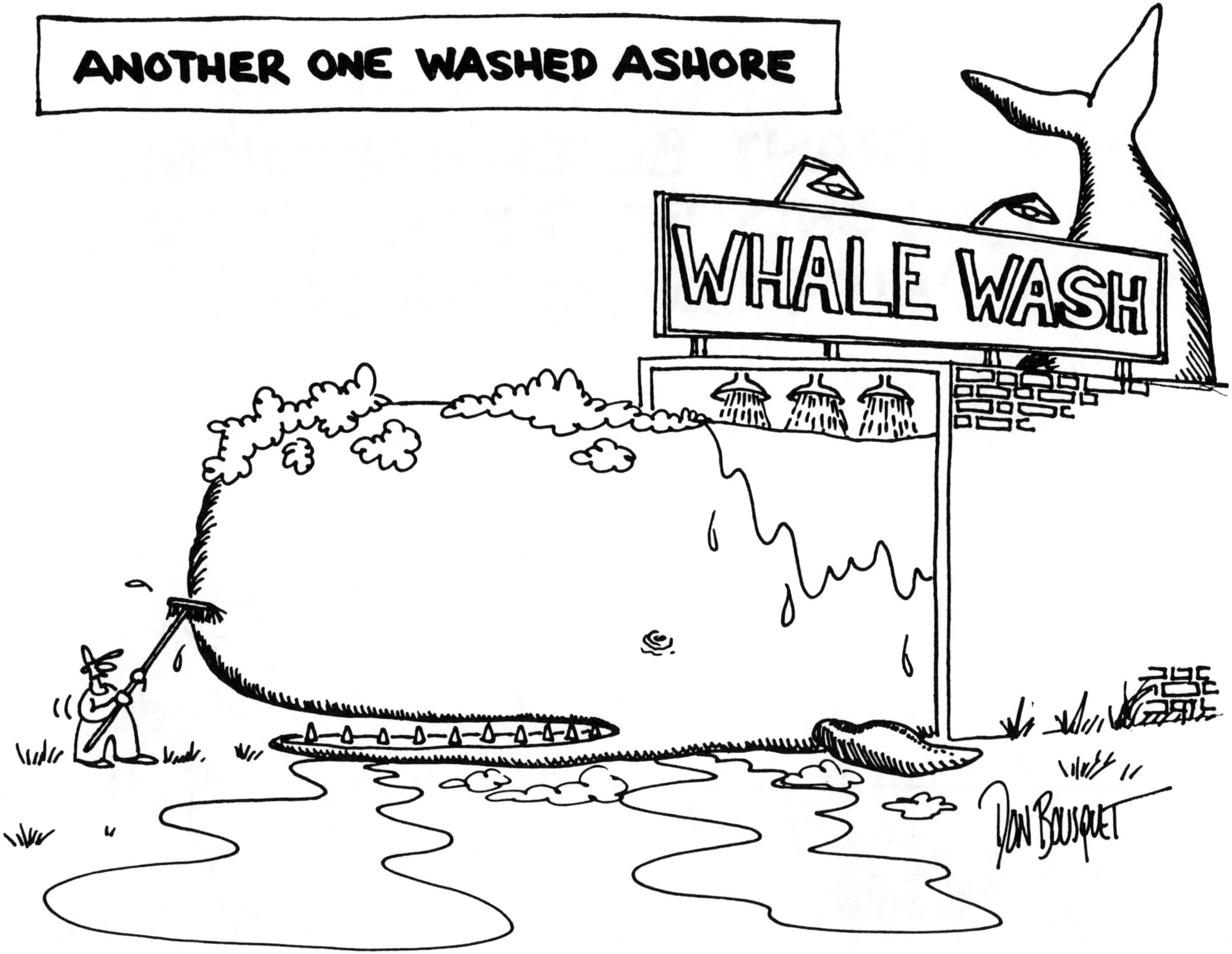
WHALE WASH
DON BOUSQUET

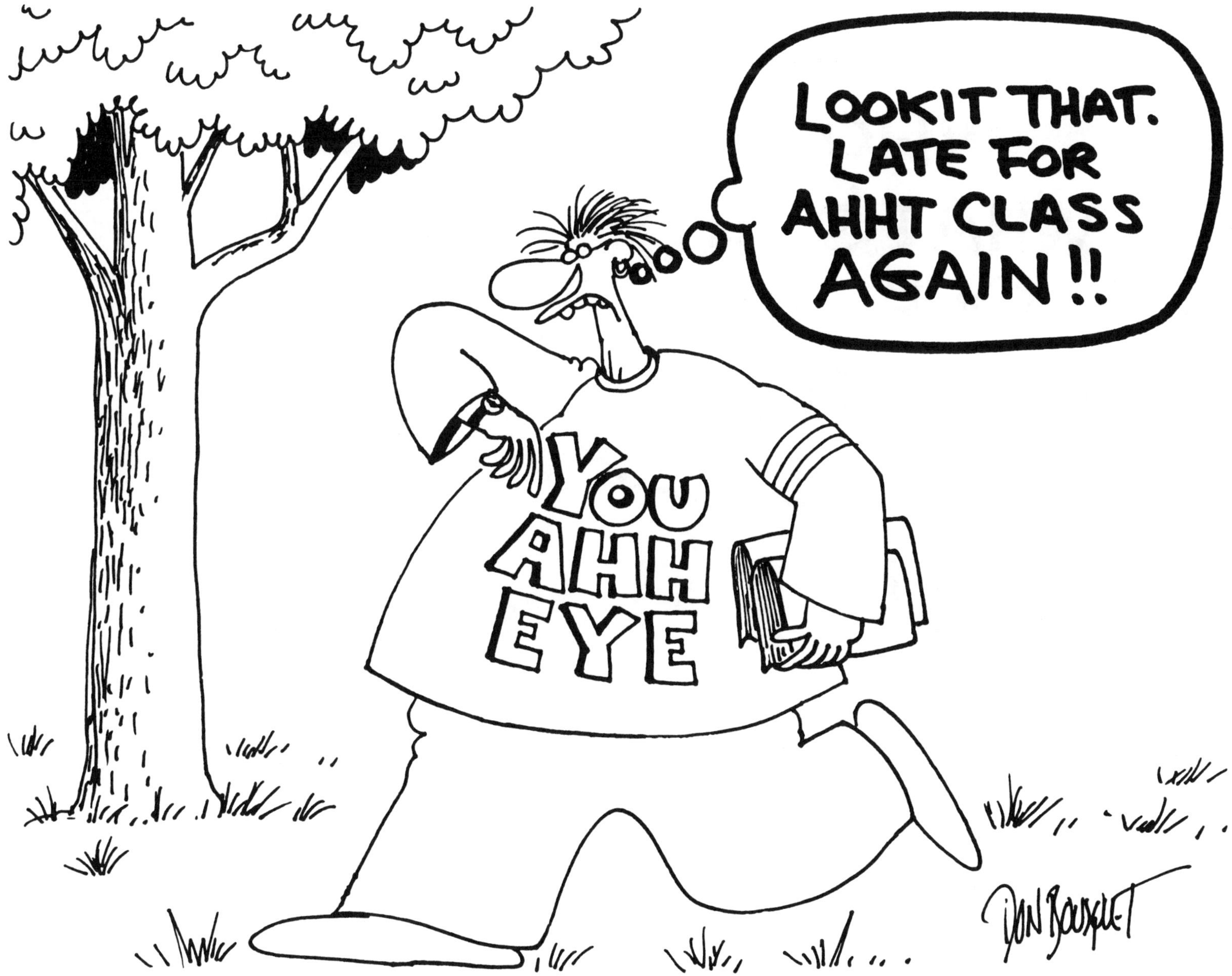
LOOKIT THAT. LATE FOR AHHT CLASS AGAIN!!
YOU AHH EYE
DON BOUSQUET

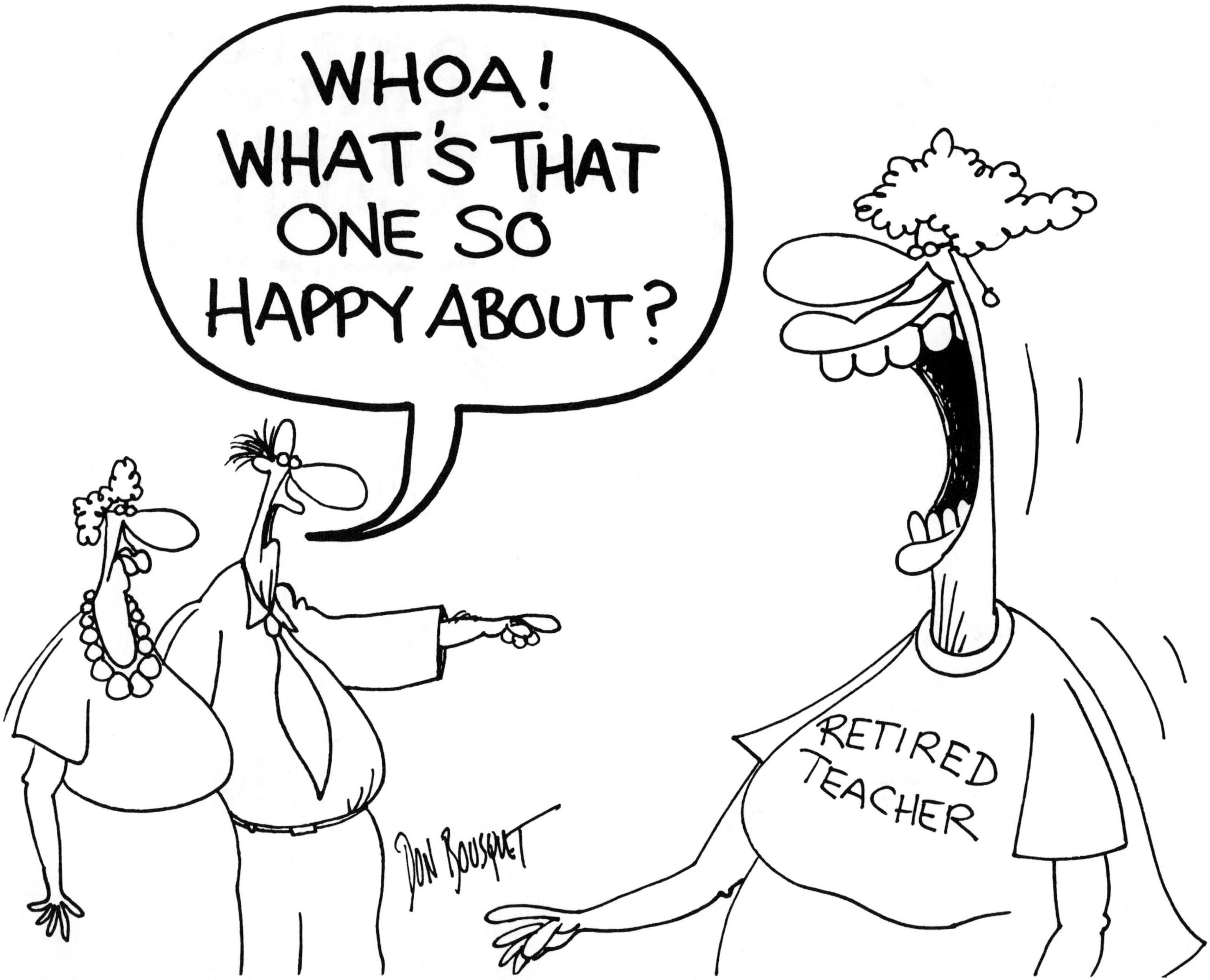
WHOA! WHAT'S THAT ONE SO HAPPY ABOUT?
RETIRED TEACHER
DON BOUSQUET

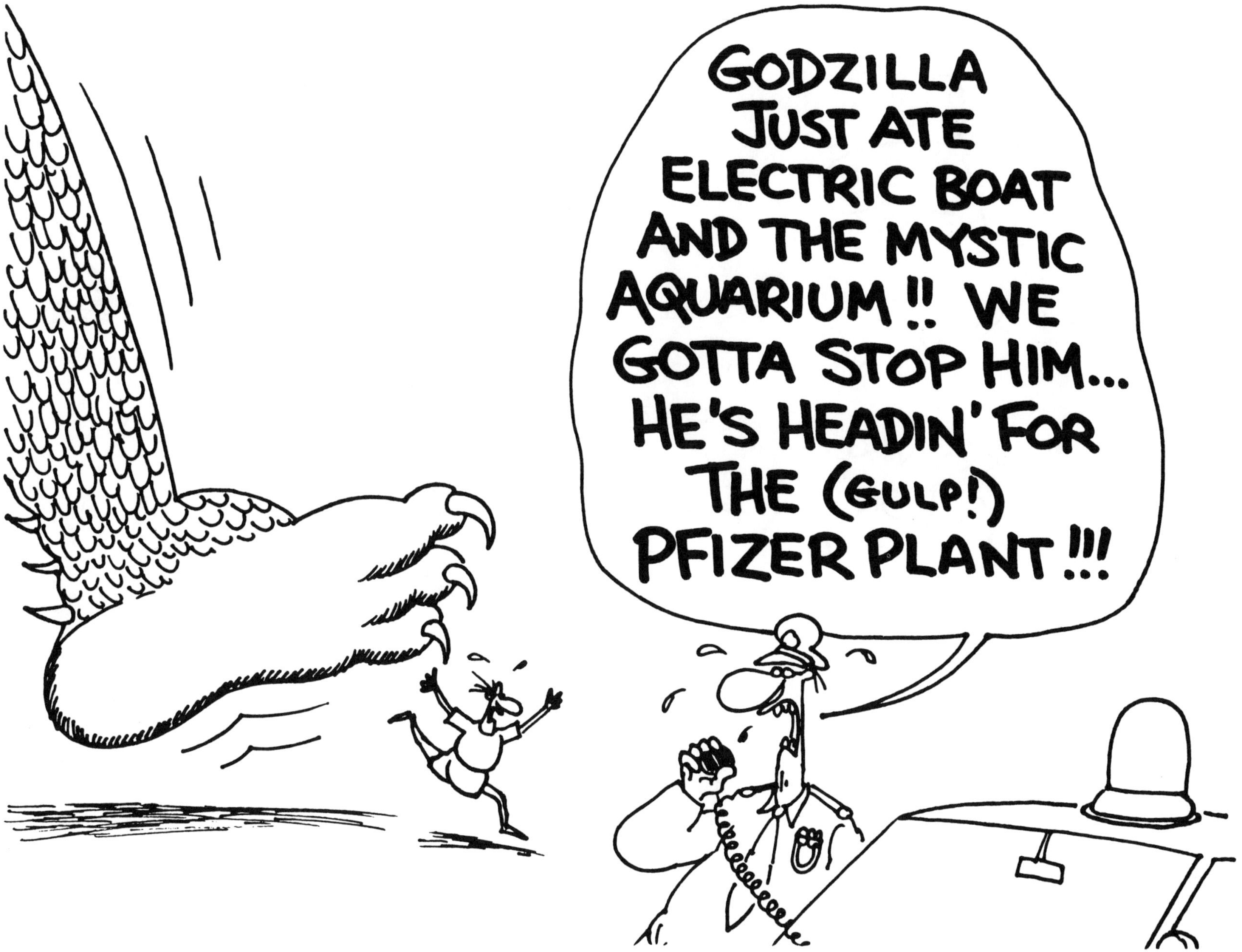
GODZILLA JUST ATE ELECTRIC BOAT AND THE MYSTIC AQUARIUM!! WE GOTTA STOP HIM... HE'S HEADIN' FOR THE (GULP!) PFIZER PLANT!!!

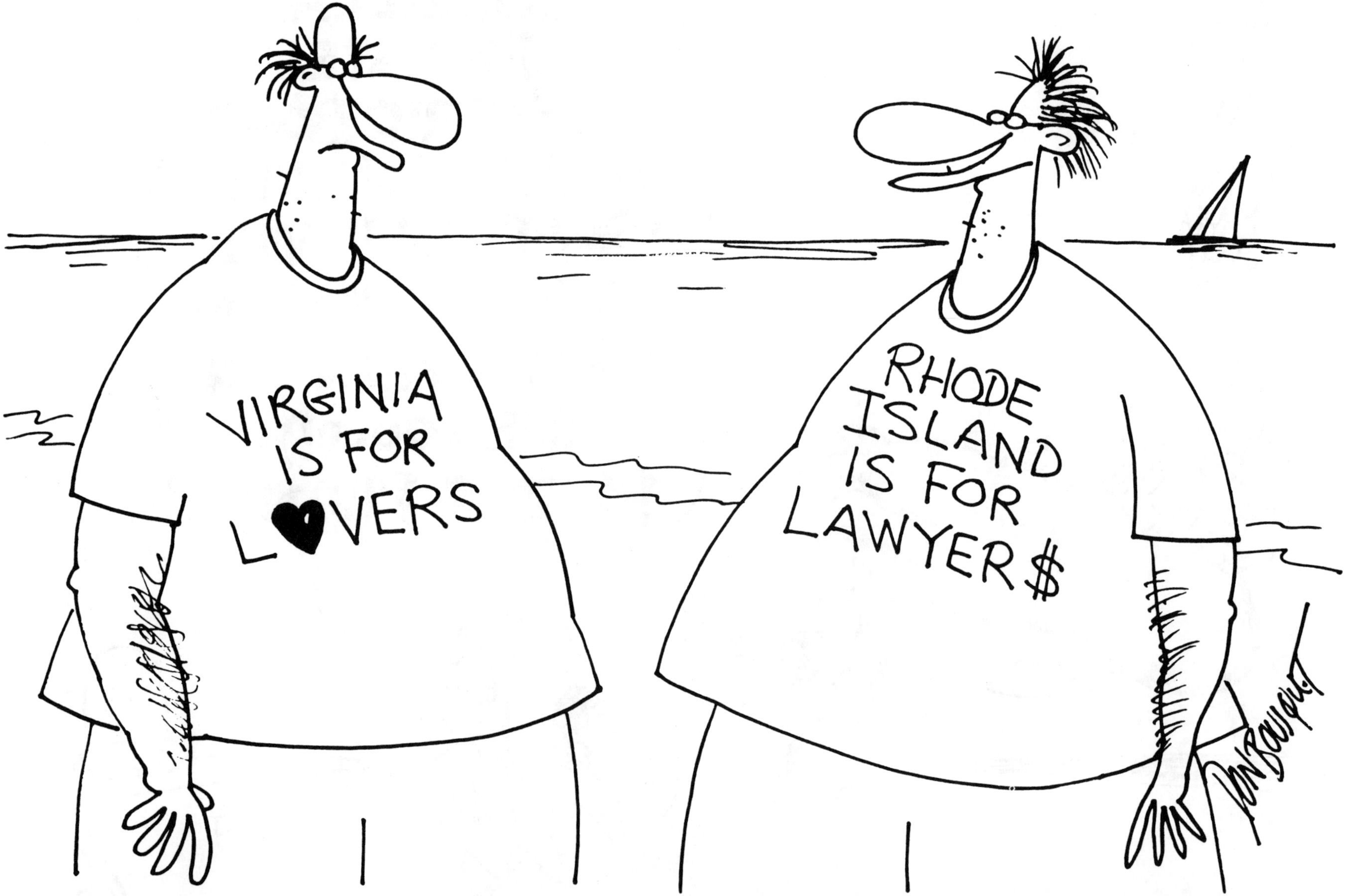
VIRGINIA IS FOR LOVERS
RHODE ISLAND IS FOR LAWYER$
DON BOUSQUET

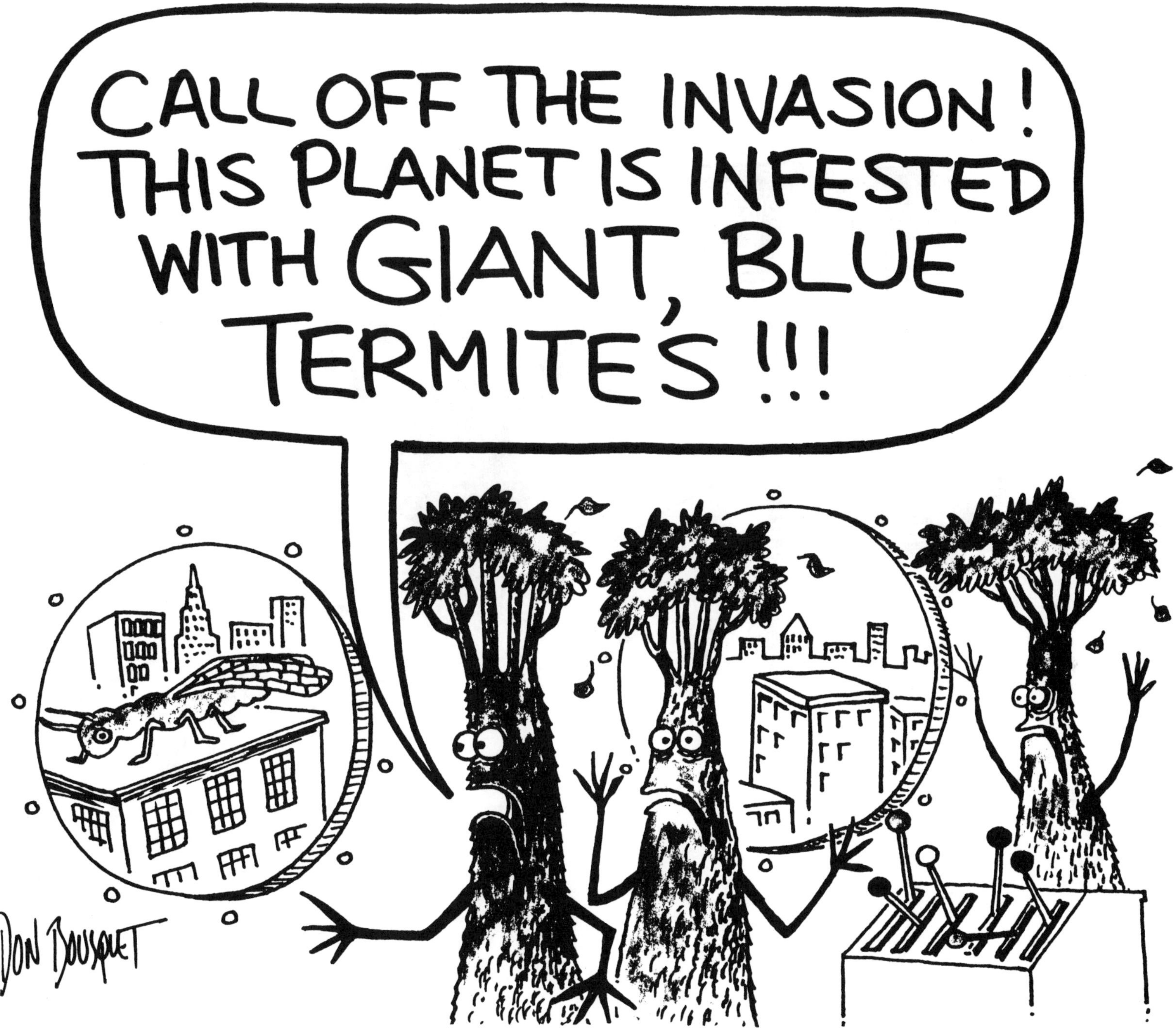
CALL OFF THE INVASION! THIS PLANET IS INFESTED WITH GIANT, BLUE TERMITE'S !!!
DON BOUSQUET

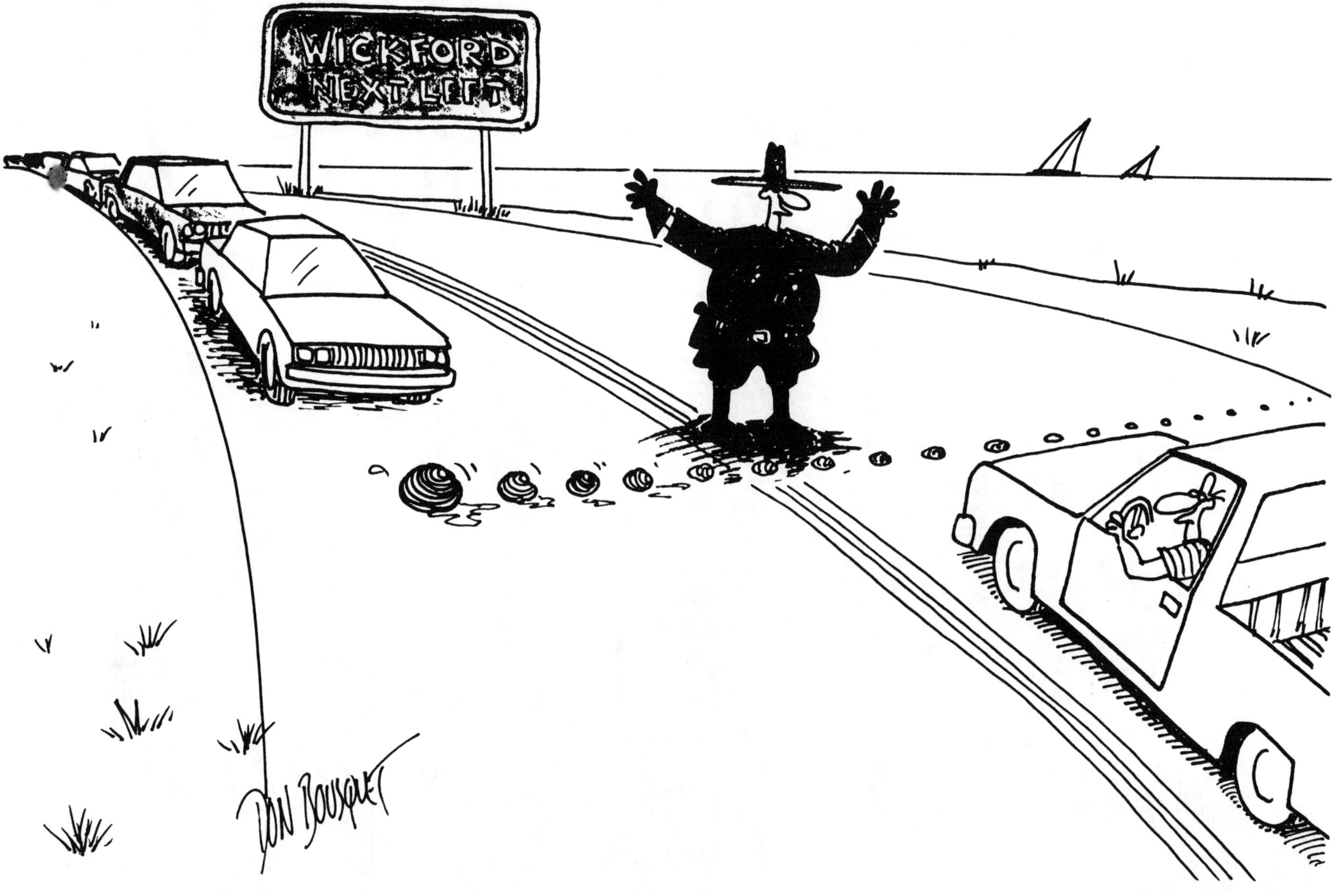
WICKFORD
NEXT LEFT
DON BOUSQUET

THE SOUND OF MILDEW GROWING ON OUR BODIES KEPT ME AWAKE AGAIN LAST NIGHT.

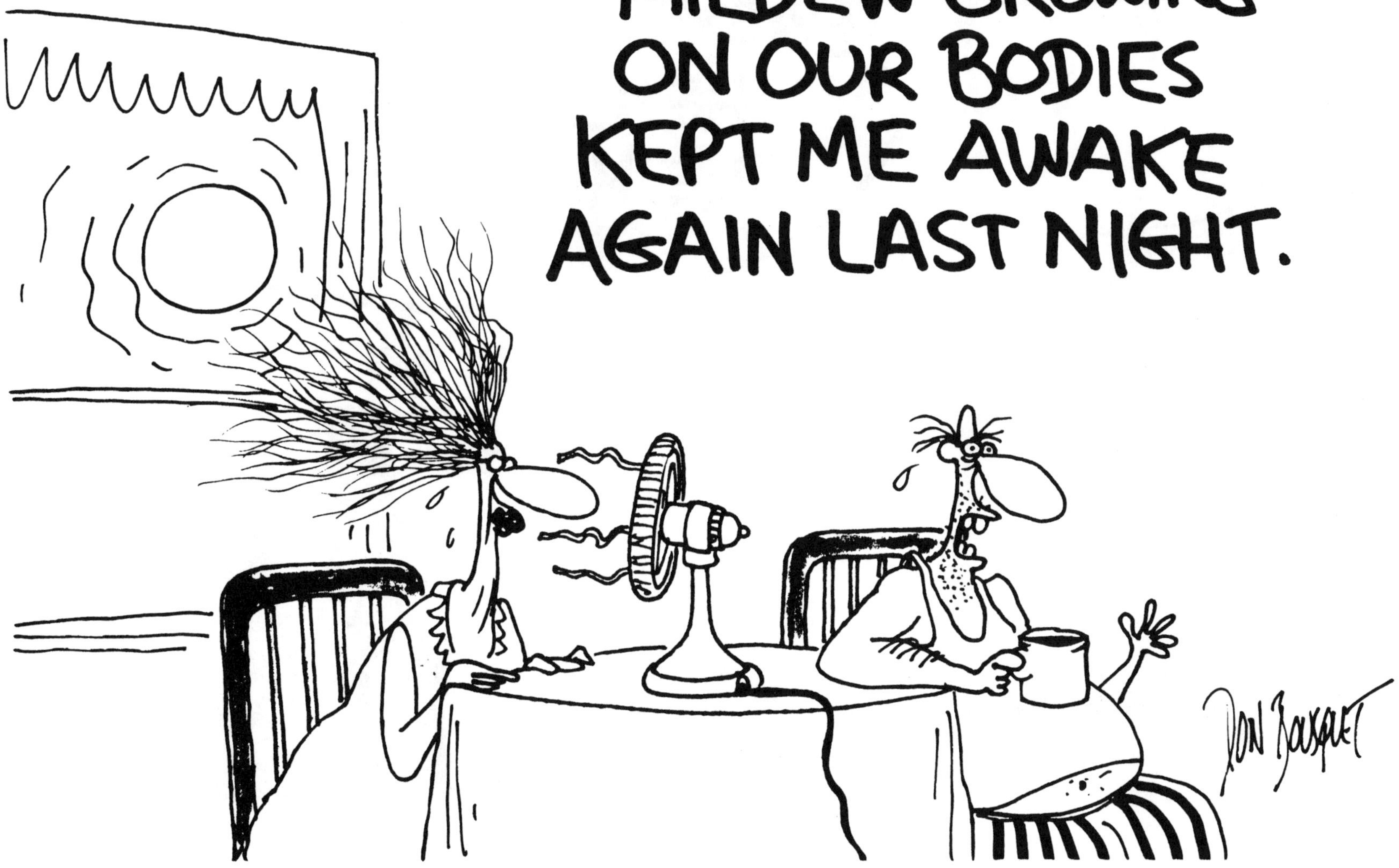
DON BOUSQUET

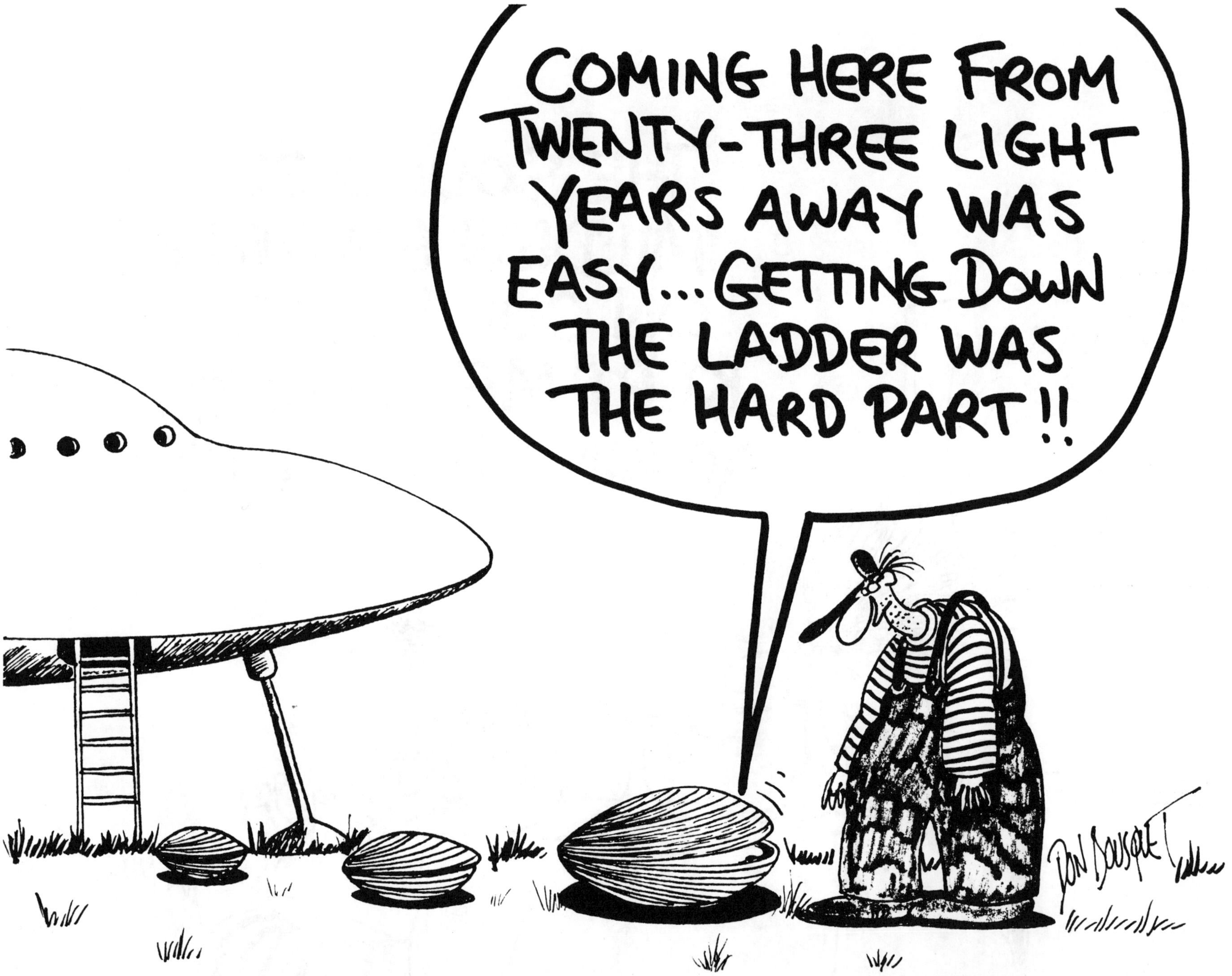
COMING HERE FROM TWENTY-THREE LIGHT YEARS AWAY WAS EASY... GETTING DOWN THE LADDER WAS THE HARD PART!!
DON DOUSQUET

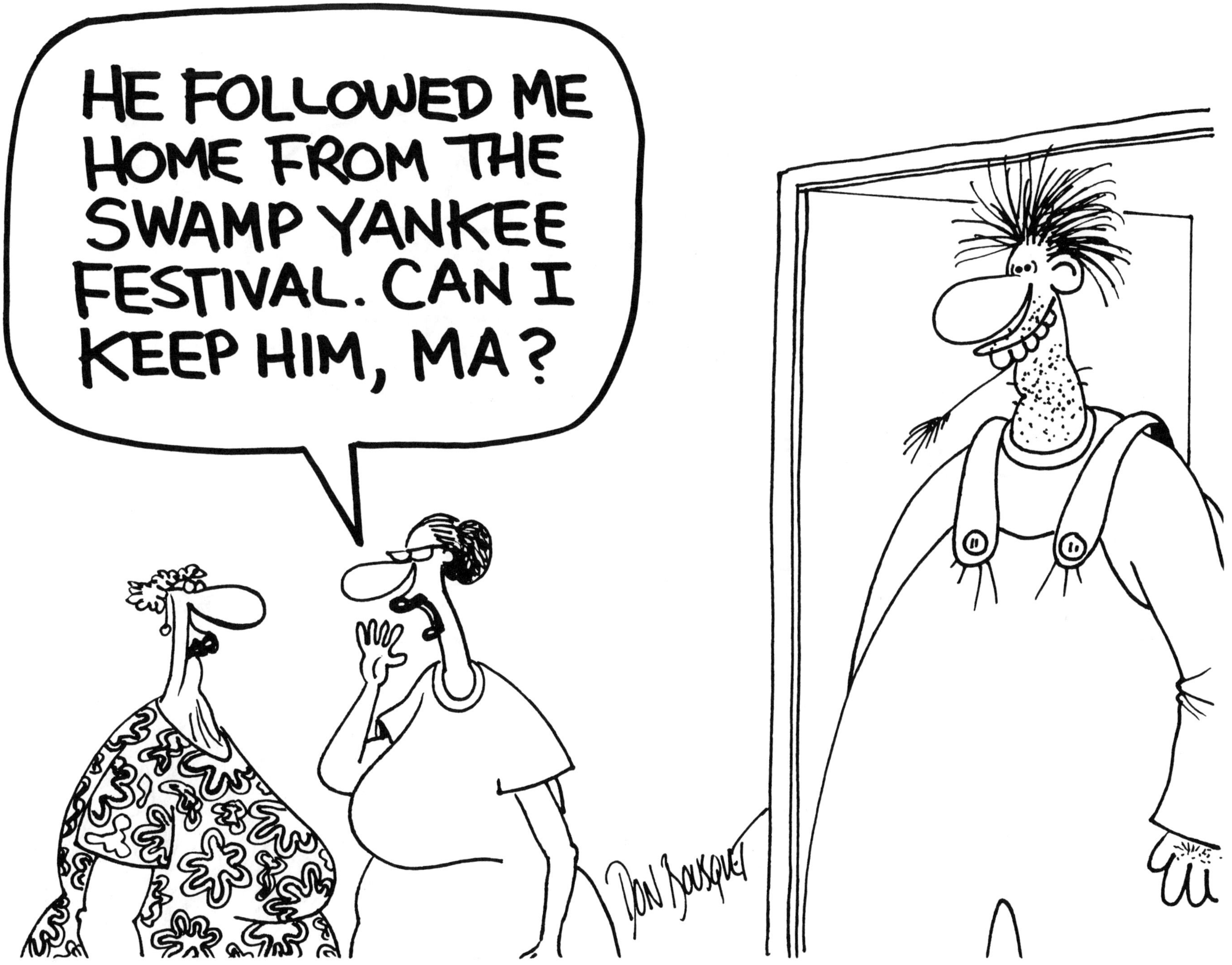
HE FOLLOWED ME HOME FROM THE SWAMP YANKEE FESTIVAL. CAN I KEEP HIM, MA?
DON BOUSQUET

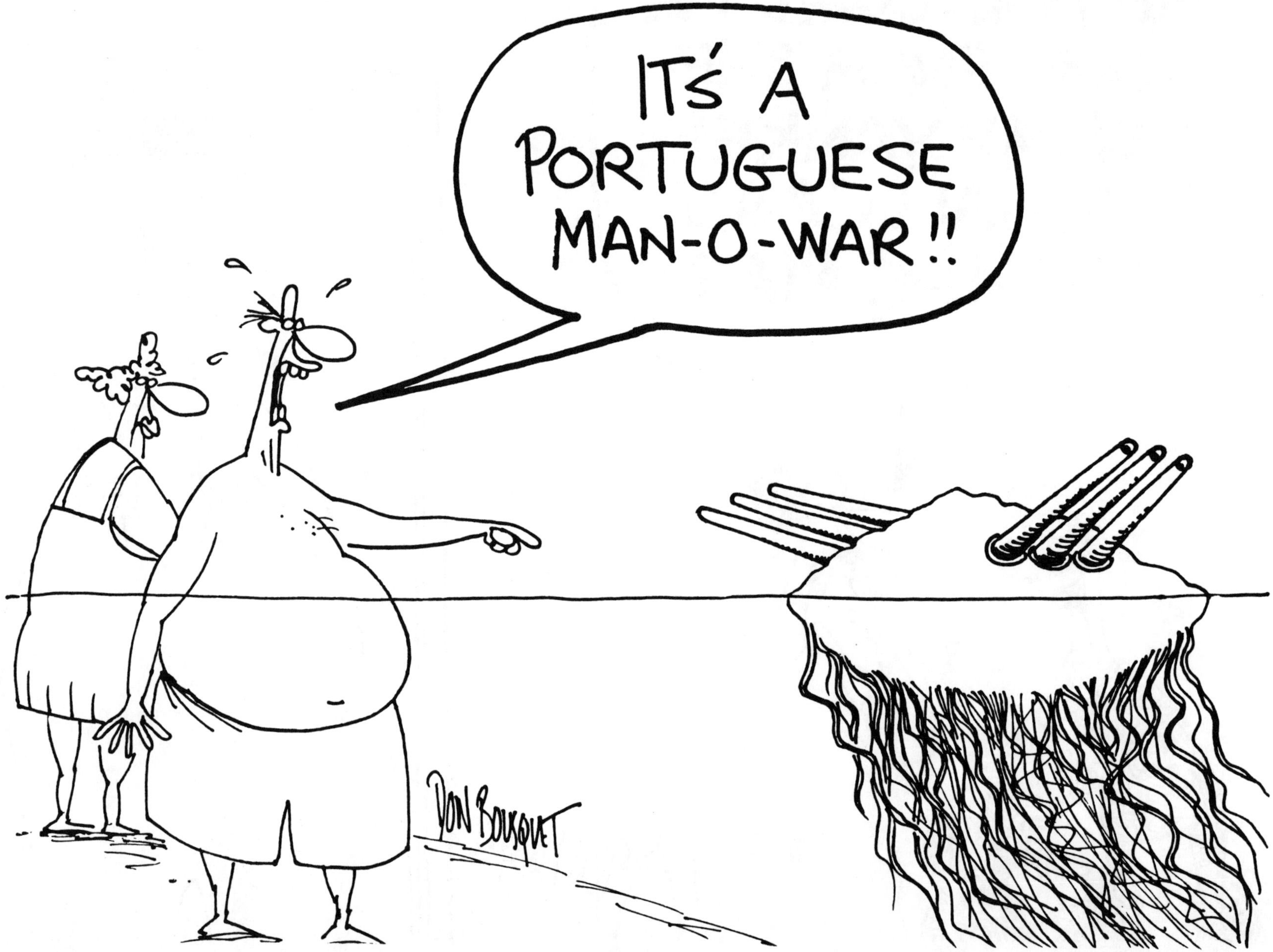
IT'S A PORTUGUESE MAN-O-WAR!!
DON BOUSQUET

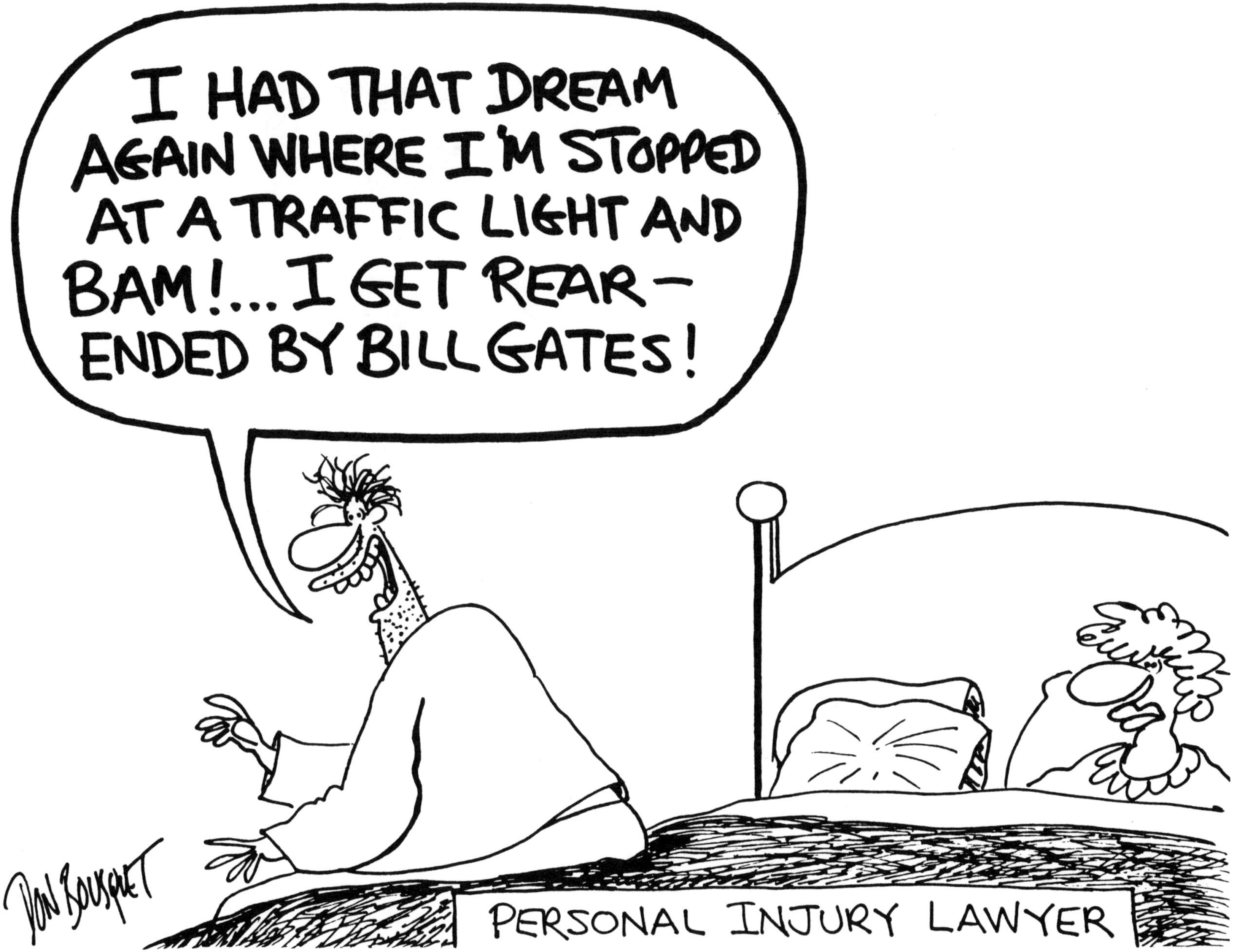
I HAD THAT DREAM AGAIN WHERE I'M STOPPED AT A TRAFFIC LIGHT AND BAM!... I GET REAR-ENDED BY BILL GATES!
DON BOUSQUET
PERSONAL INJURY LAWYER

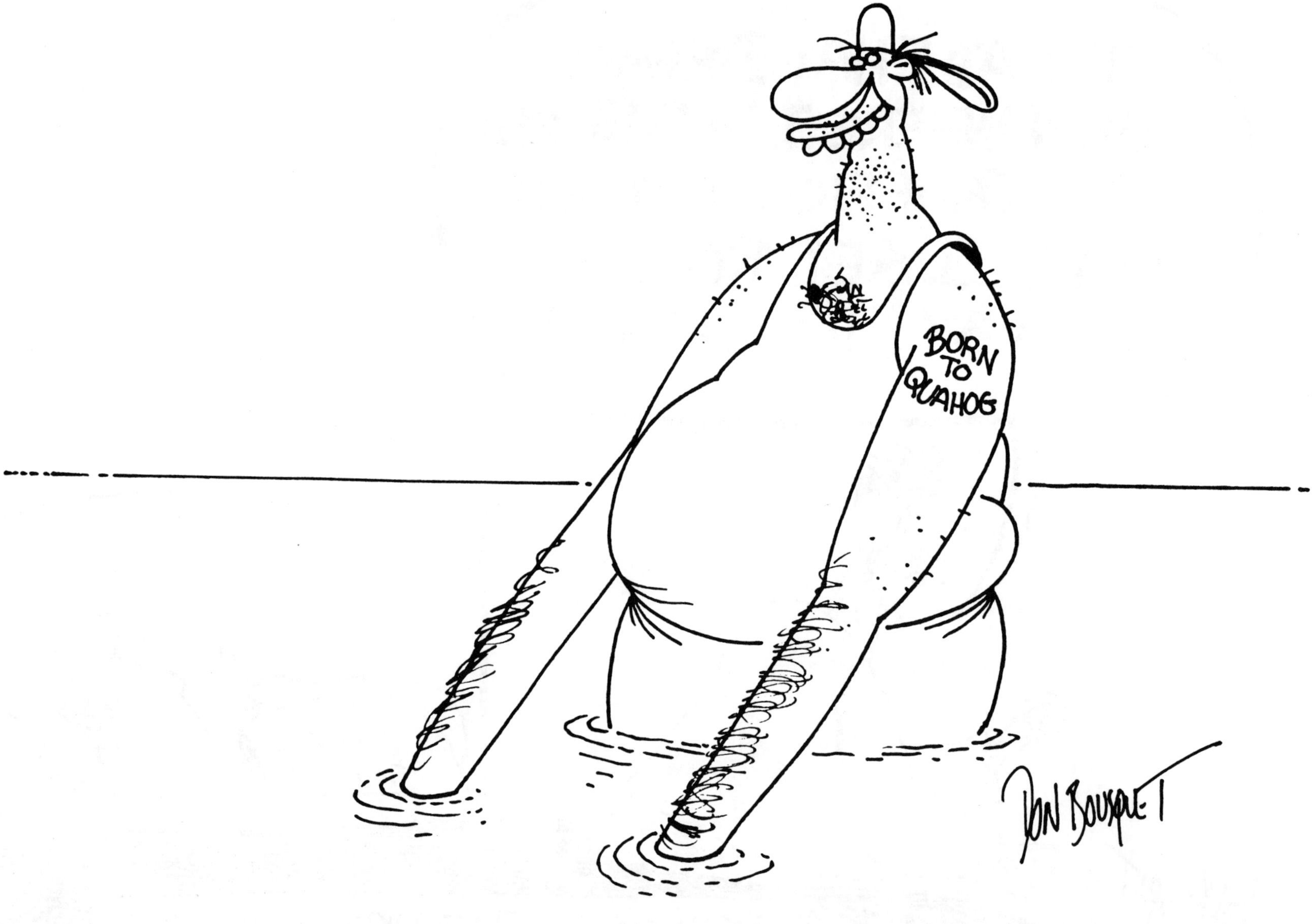
BORN TO QUAHOG
DON BOUSQUET

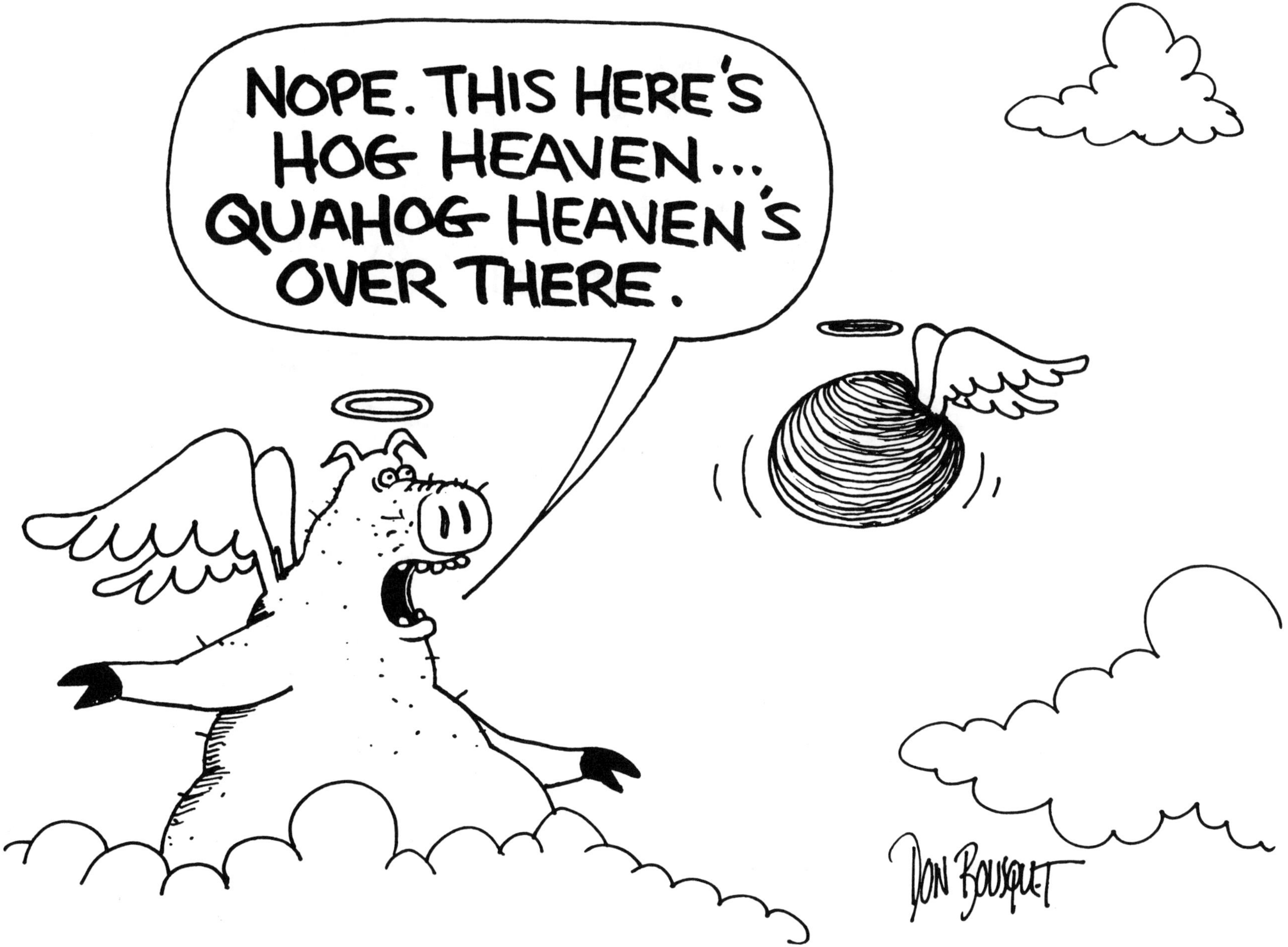
NOPE. THIS HERE'S HOG HEAVEN... QUAHOG HEAVEN'S OVER THERE.
DON BOUSQUET

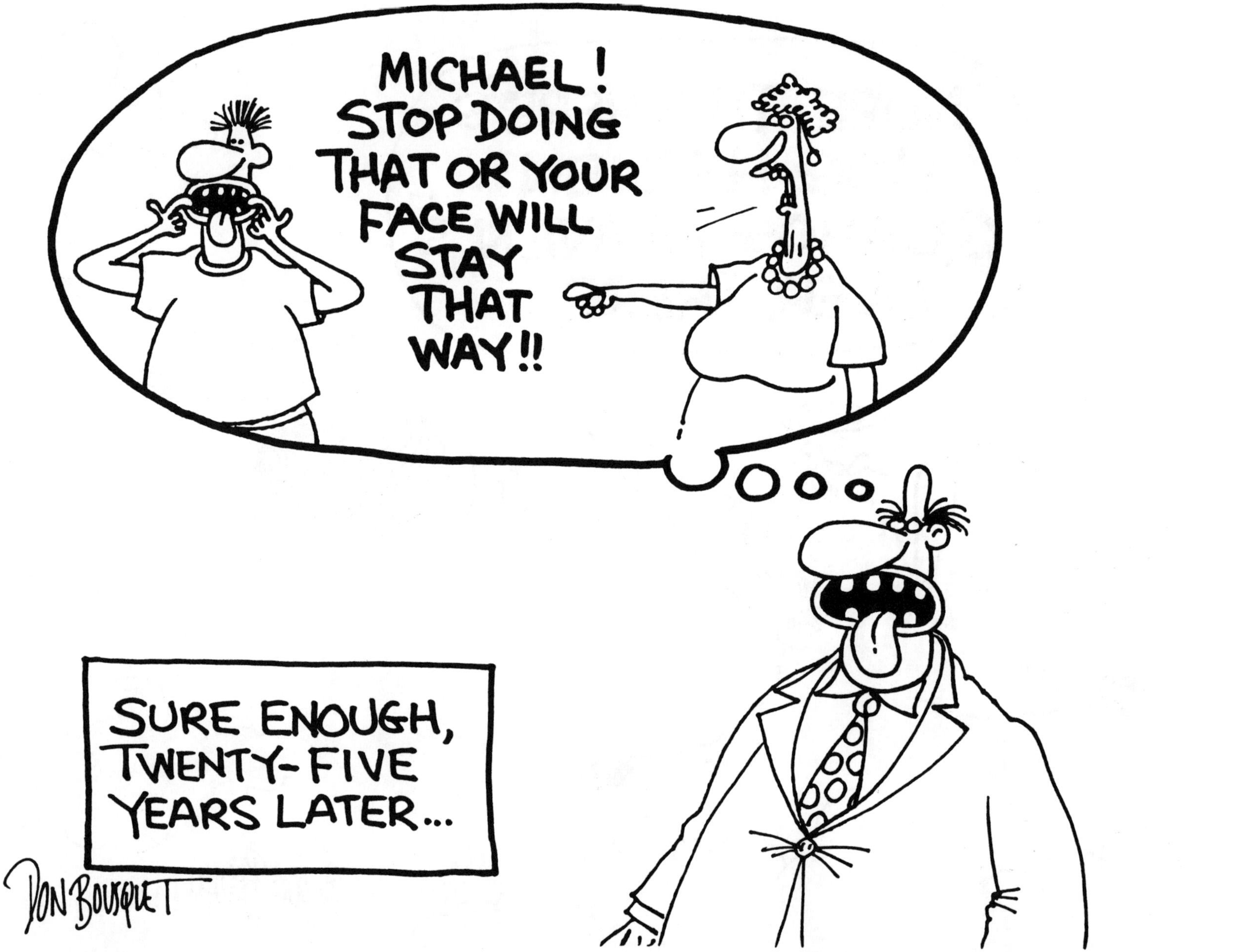
MICHAEL! STOP DOING THAT OR YOUR FACE WILL STAY THAT WAY!!
SURE ENOUGH, TWENTY-FIVE YEARS LATER...
DON BOUSQUET

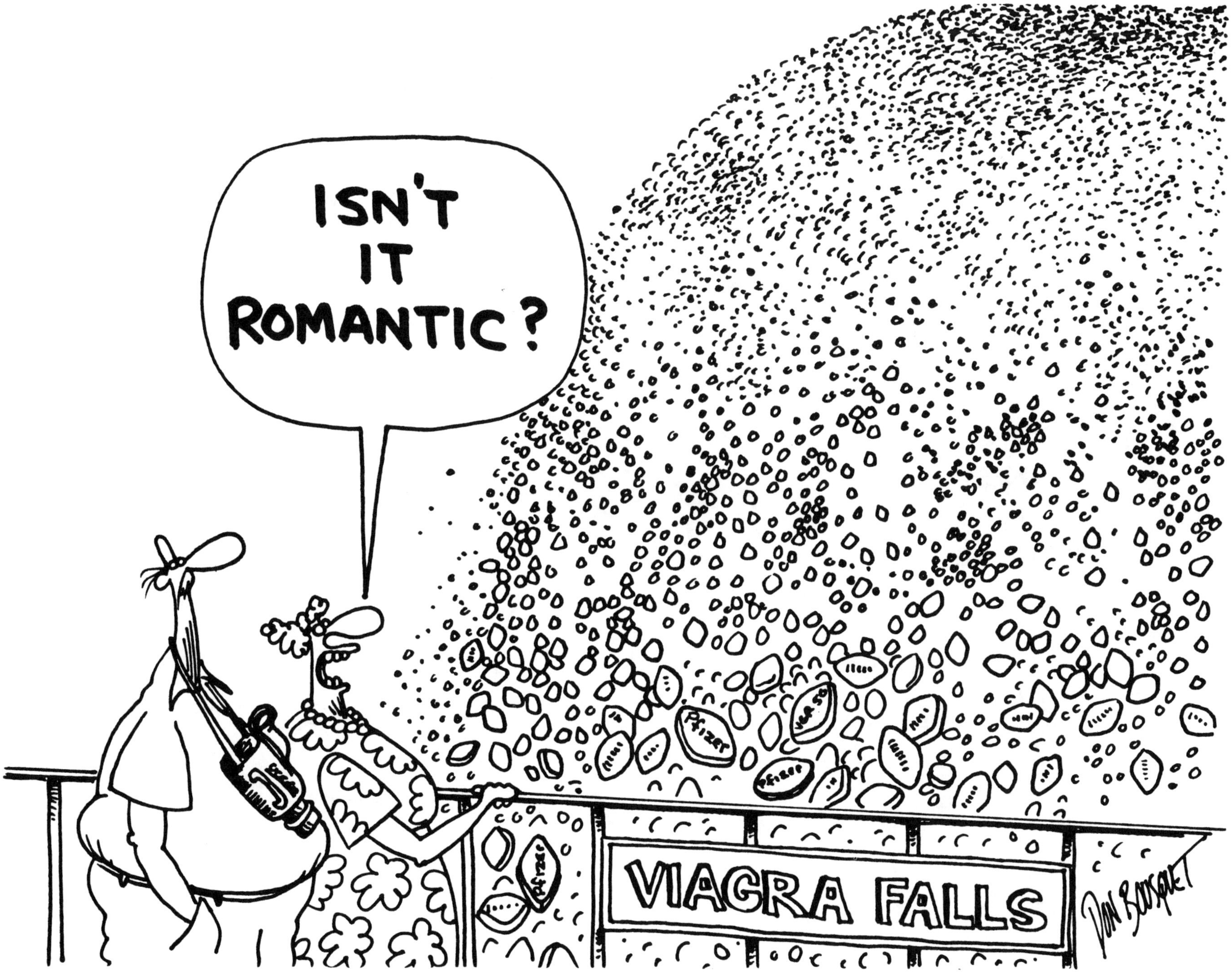
ISN'T IT ROMANTIC?
VIAGRA FALLS

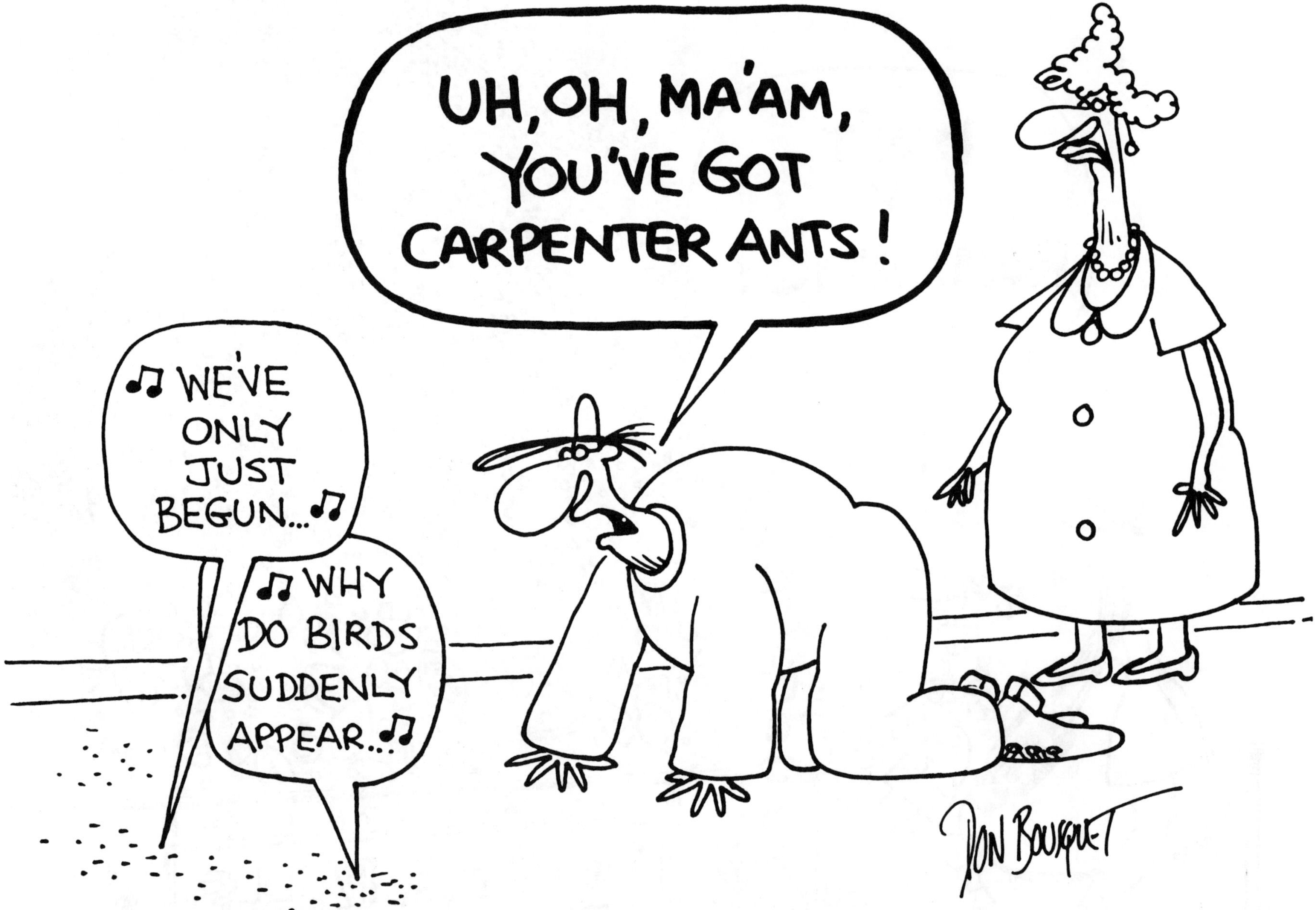
UH, OH, MA'AM, YOU'VE GOT CARPENTER ANTS!
♫ WE'VE ONLY JUST BEGUN... ♫
♫ WHY DO BIRDS SUDDENLY APPEAR... ♫
DON BOUSQUET

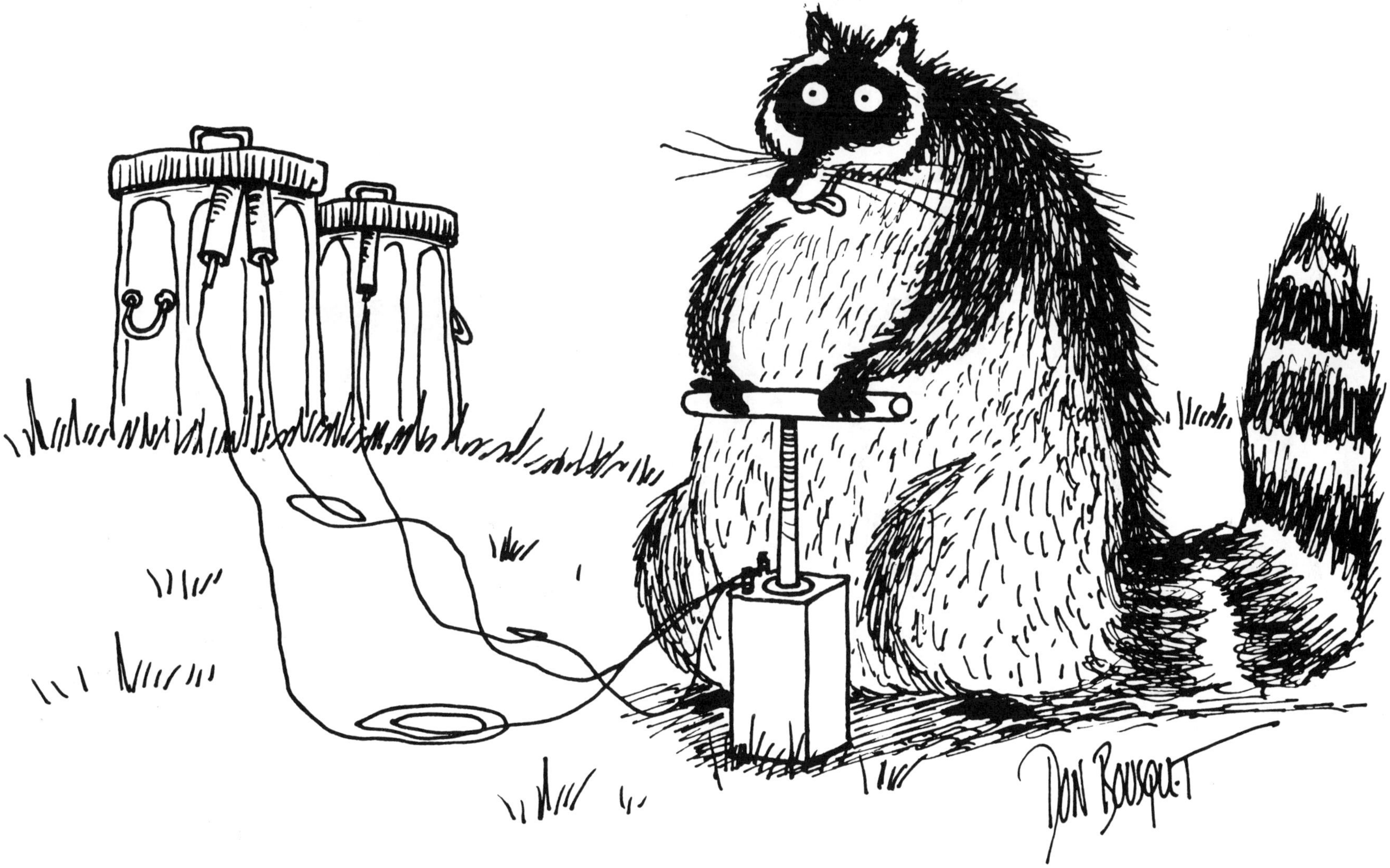
DON BOUSQUET

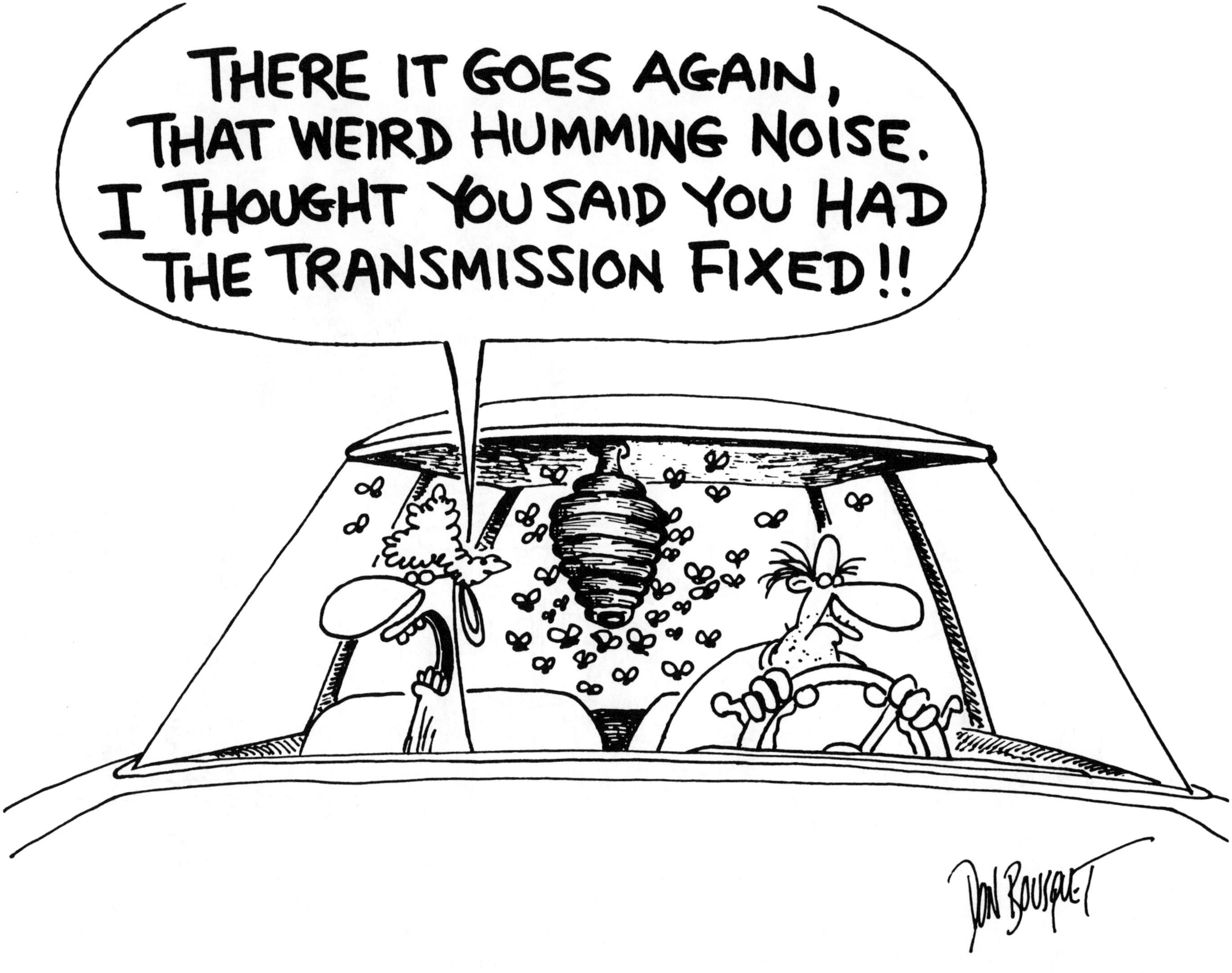
THERE IT GOES AGAIN, THAT WEIRD HUMMING NOISE. I THOUGHT YOU SAID YOU HAD THE TRANSMISSION FIXED!!
DON BOUSQUET

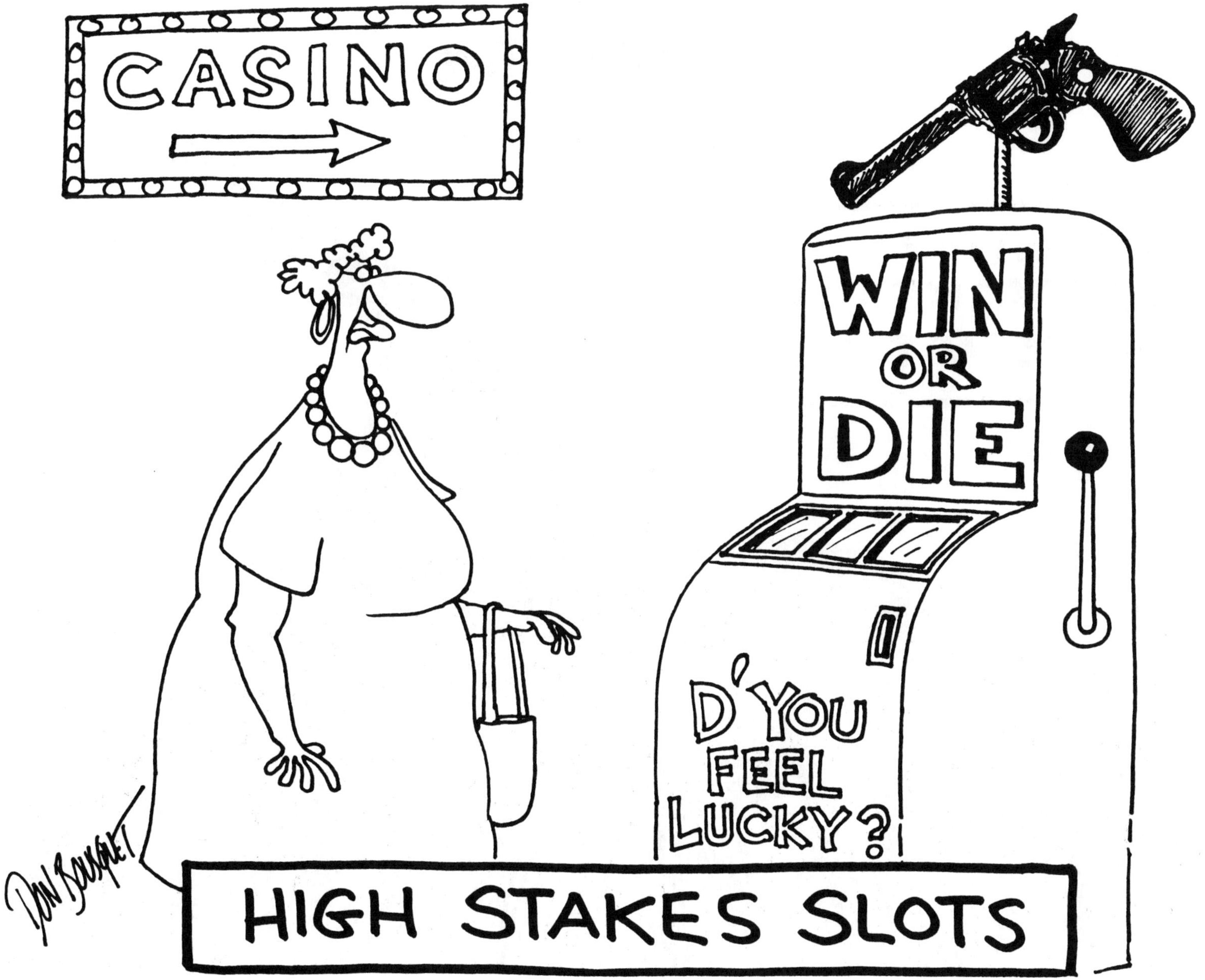
CASINO
WIN OR DIE
D'YOU FEEL LUCKY?

HIGH STAKES SLOTS

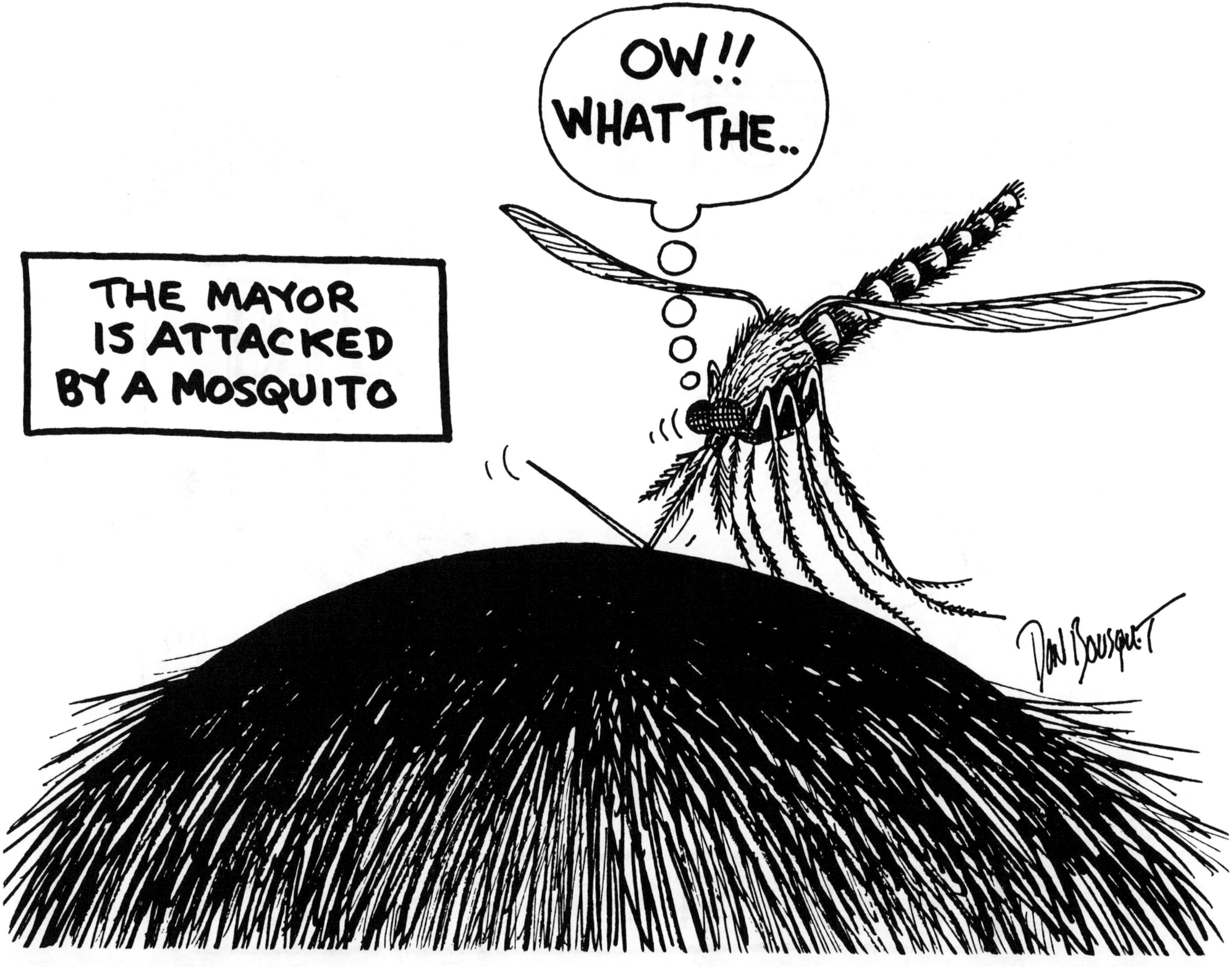
THE MAYOR IS ATTACKED BY A MOSQUITO
OW!! WHAT THE..
DAN BOUSQUET

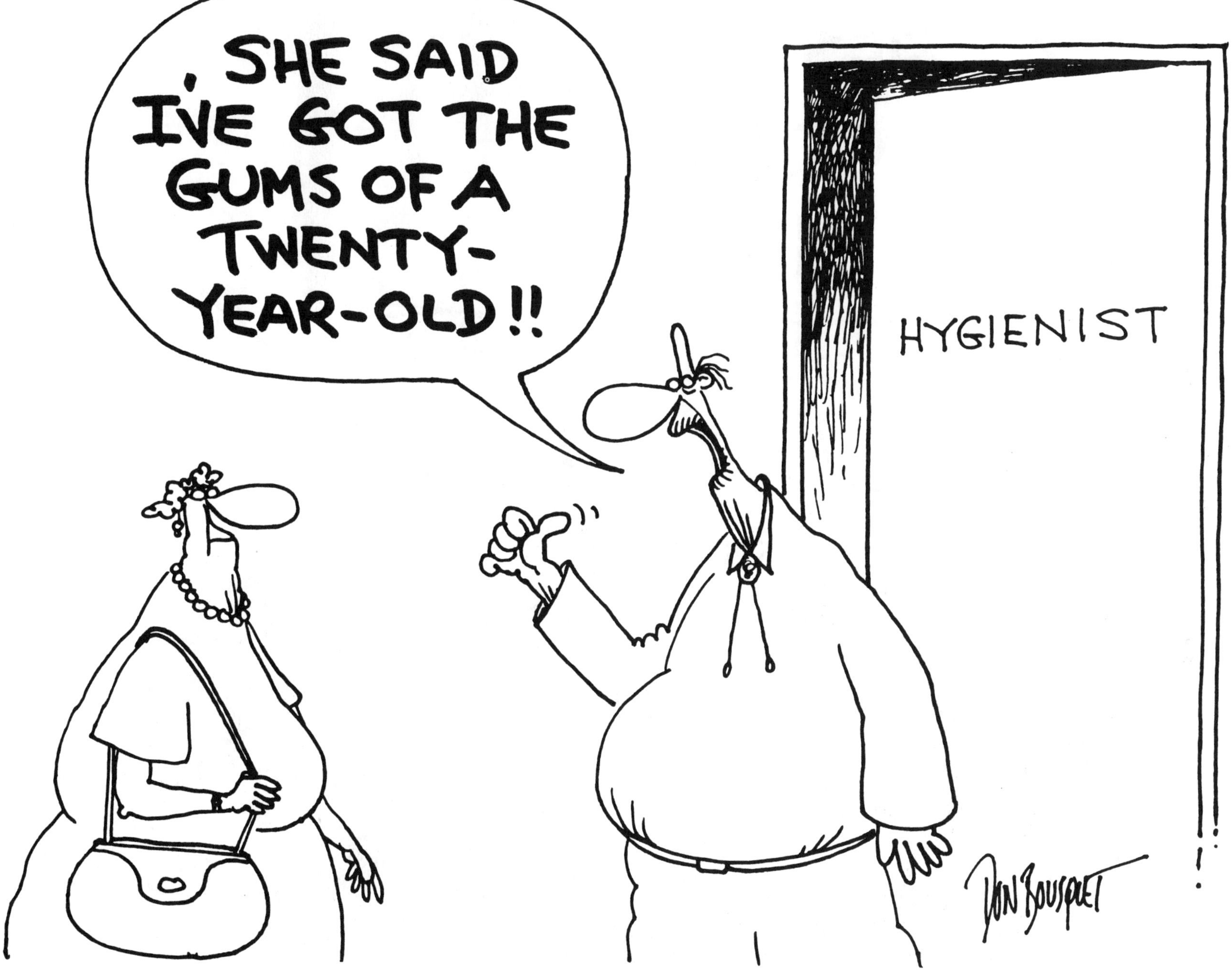
SHE SAID I'VE GOT THE GUMS OF A TWENTY-YEAR-OLD!!
HYGIENIST
DON BOUSQUET

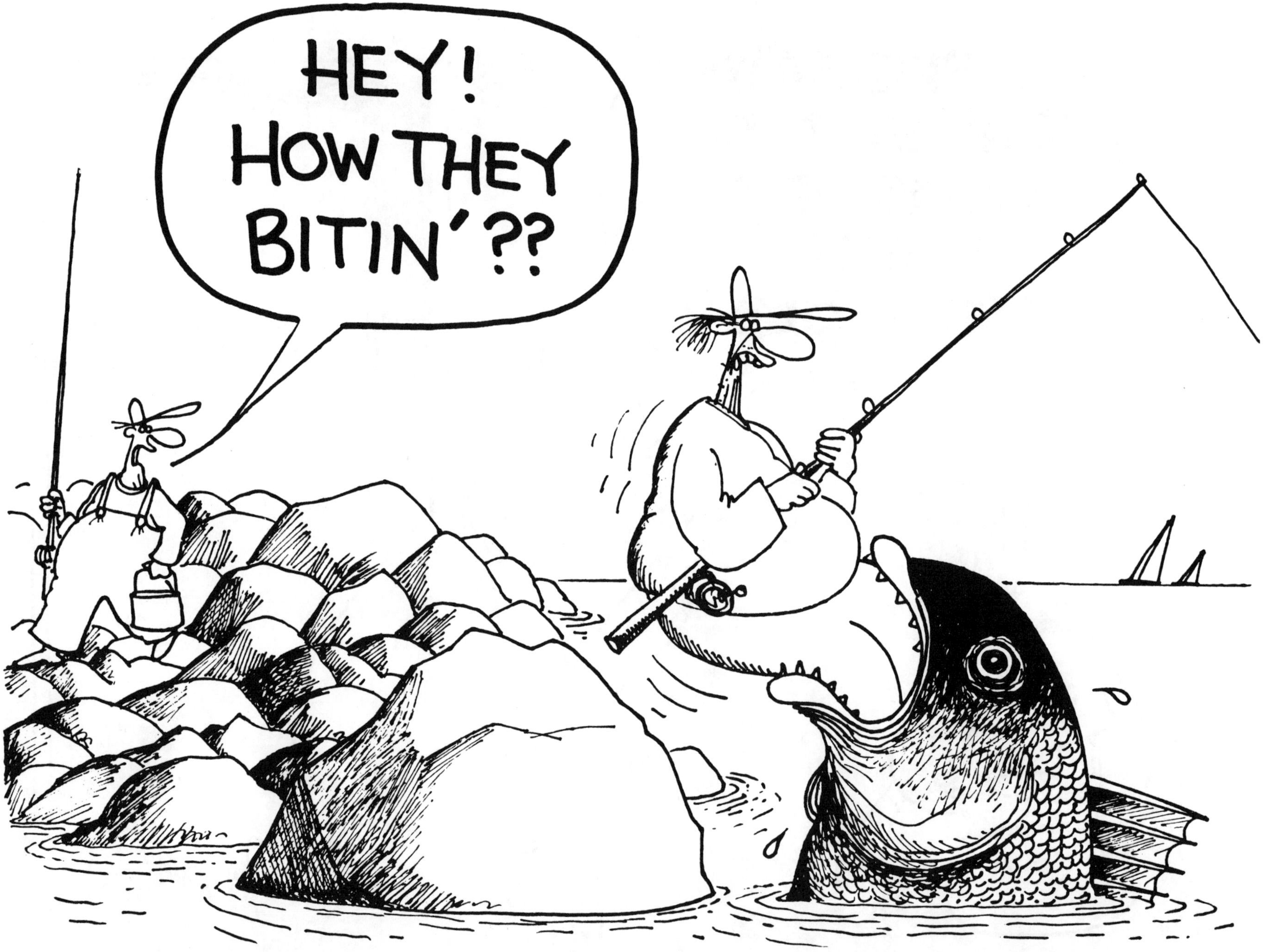
HEY! HOW THEY BITIN'??

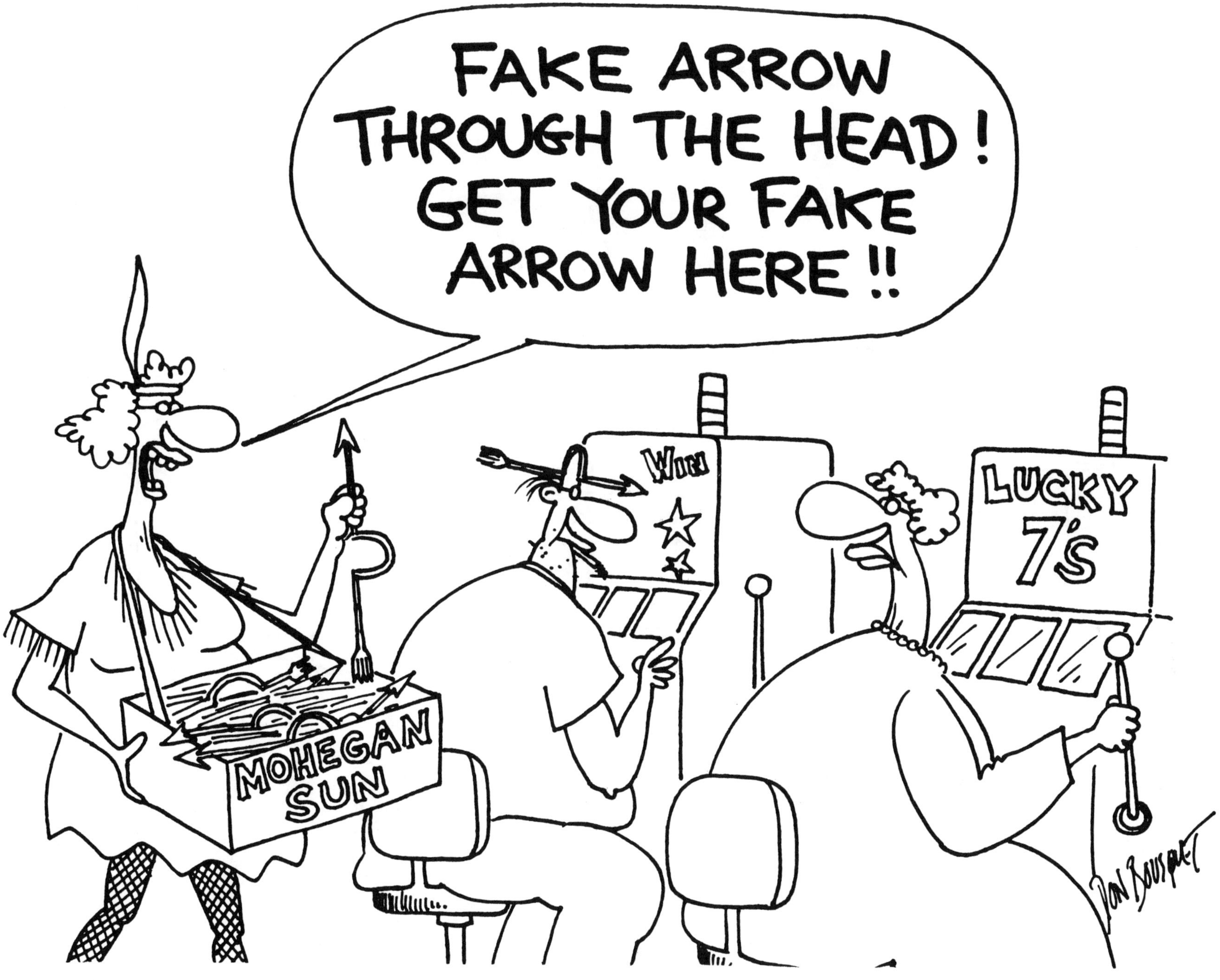
FAKE ARROW THROUGH THE HEAD! GET YOUR FAKE ARROW HERE!!
WIN
LUCKY 7'S
MOHEGAN SUN
DON BOUSQUET

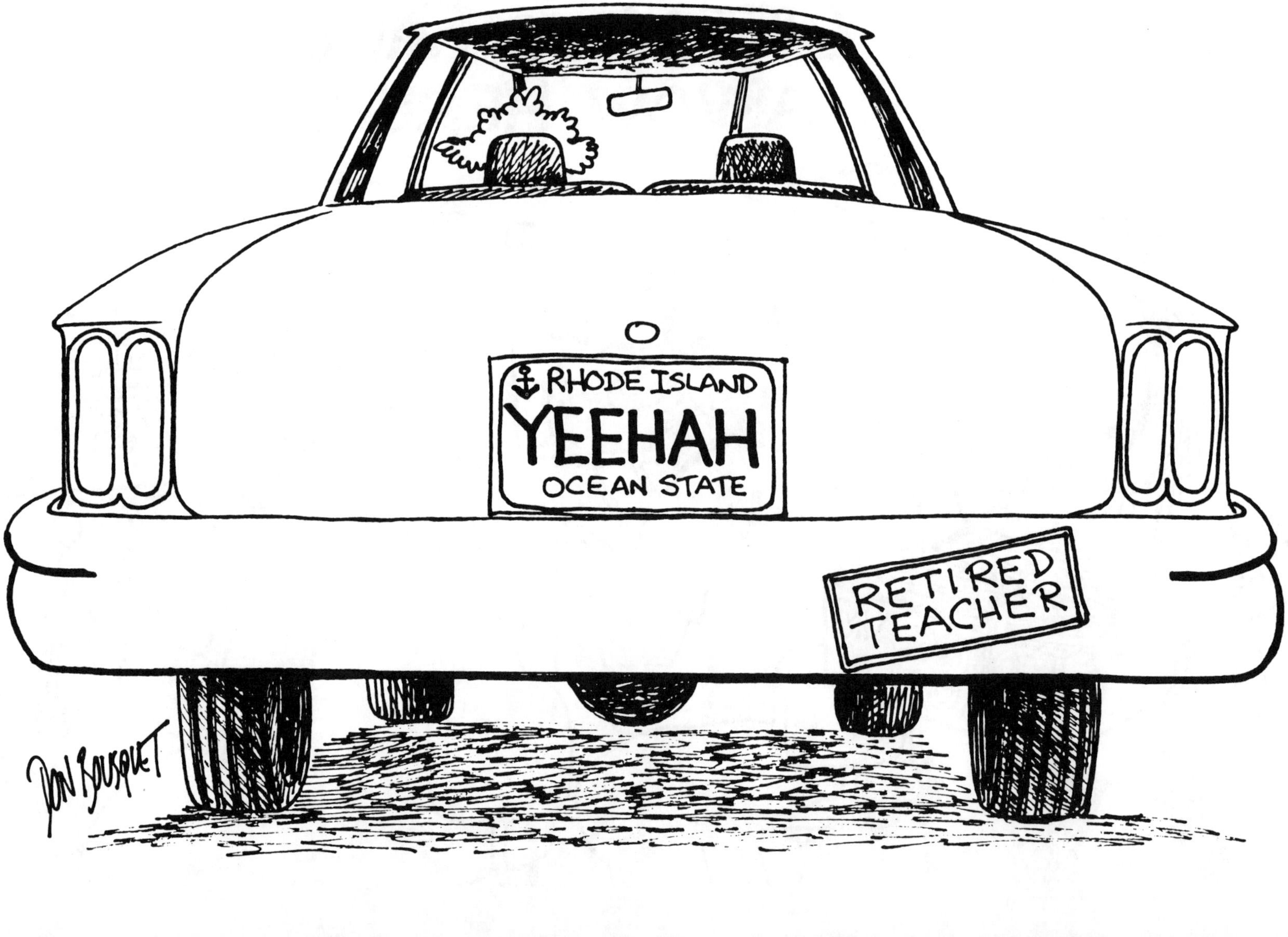
RHODE ISLAND
YEEHAH
OCEAN STATE
RETIRED TEACHER
DON BOUSQUET

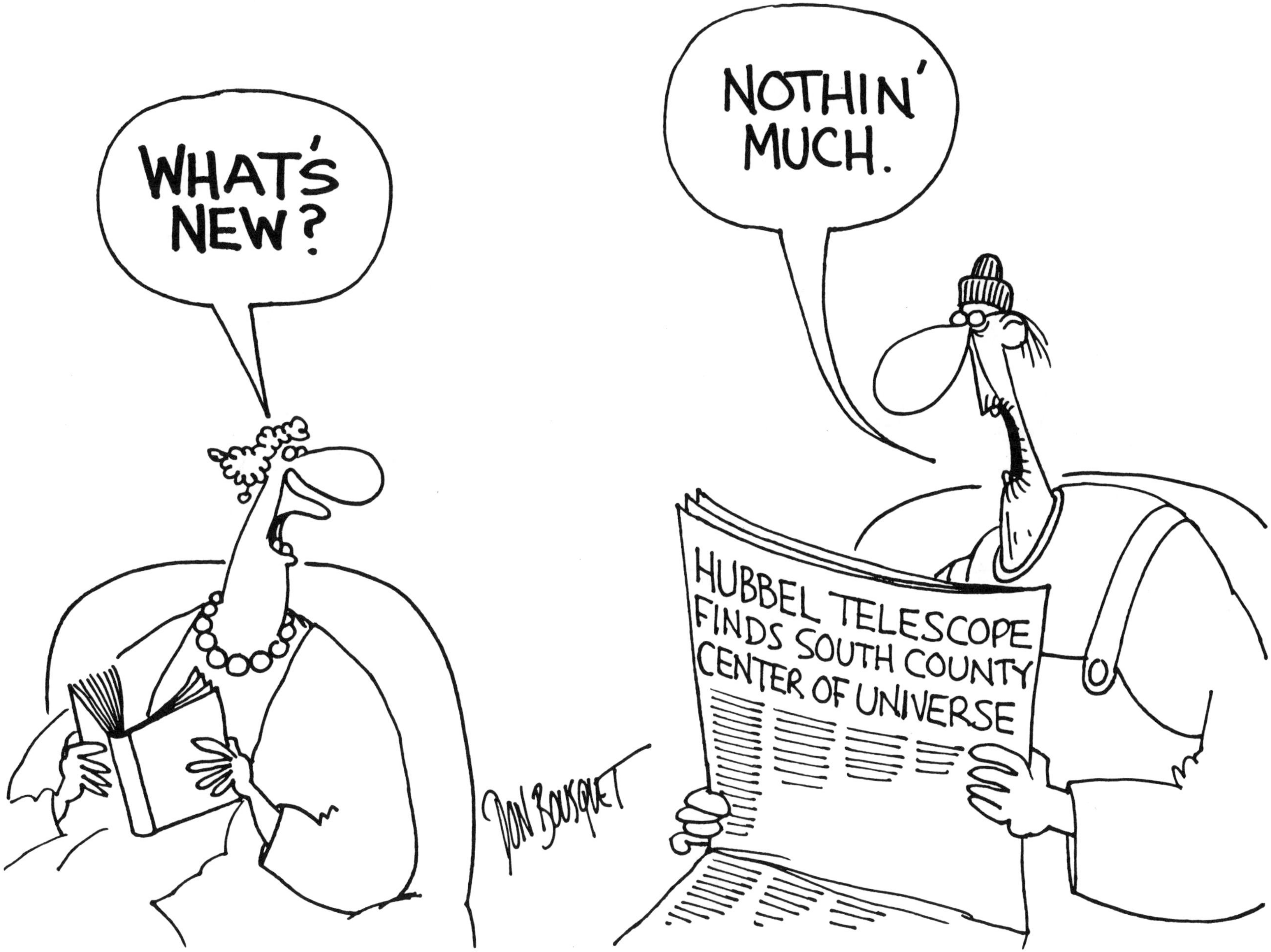
WHAT'S NEW?
NOTHIN' MUCH.
HUBBEL TELESCOPE FINDS SOUTH COUNTY CENTER OF UNIVERSE
DON BOUSQUET

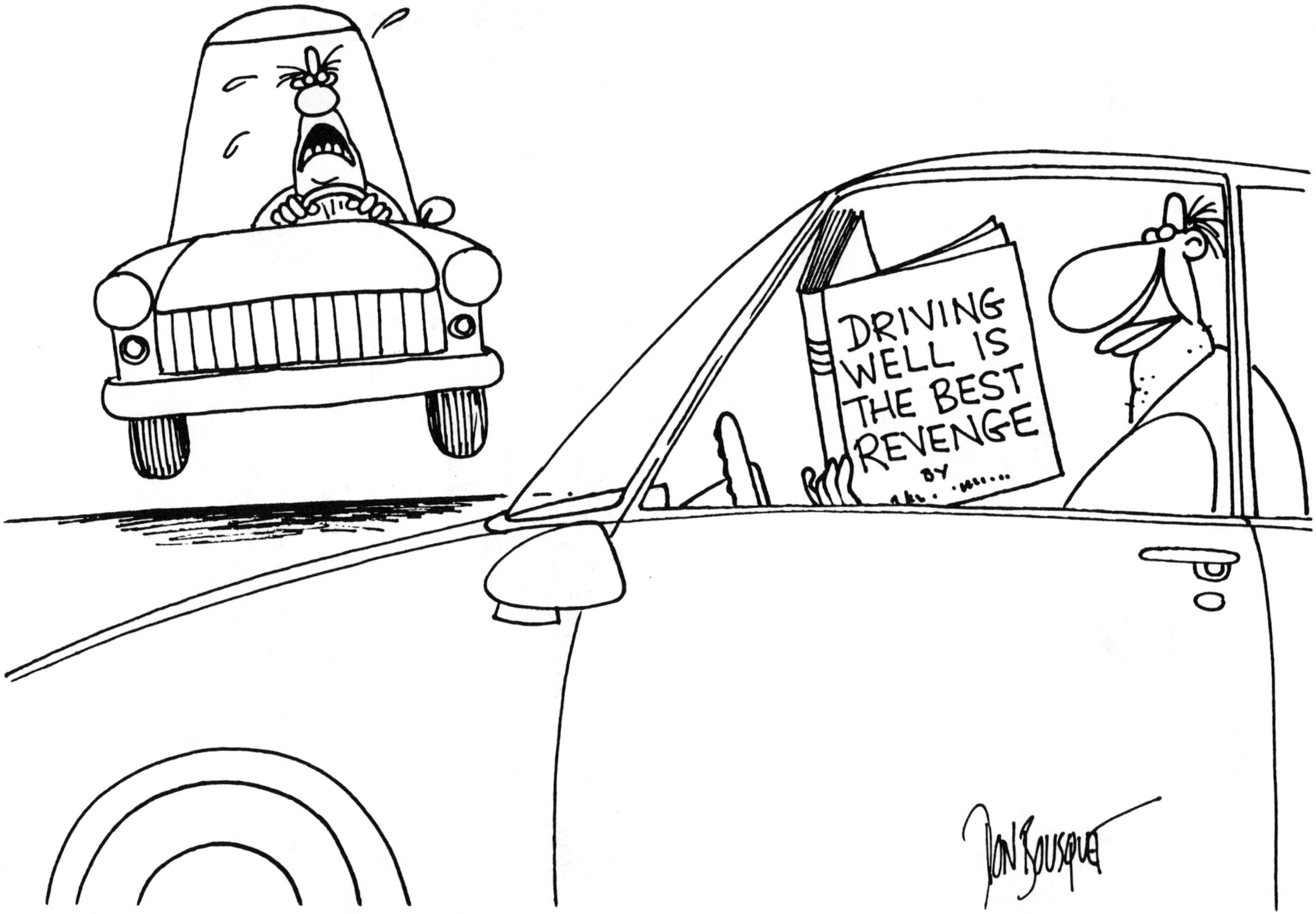
DRIVING WELL IS THE BEST REVENGE
BY
DON BOUSQUET

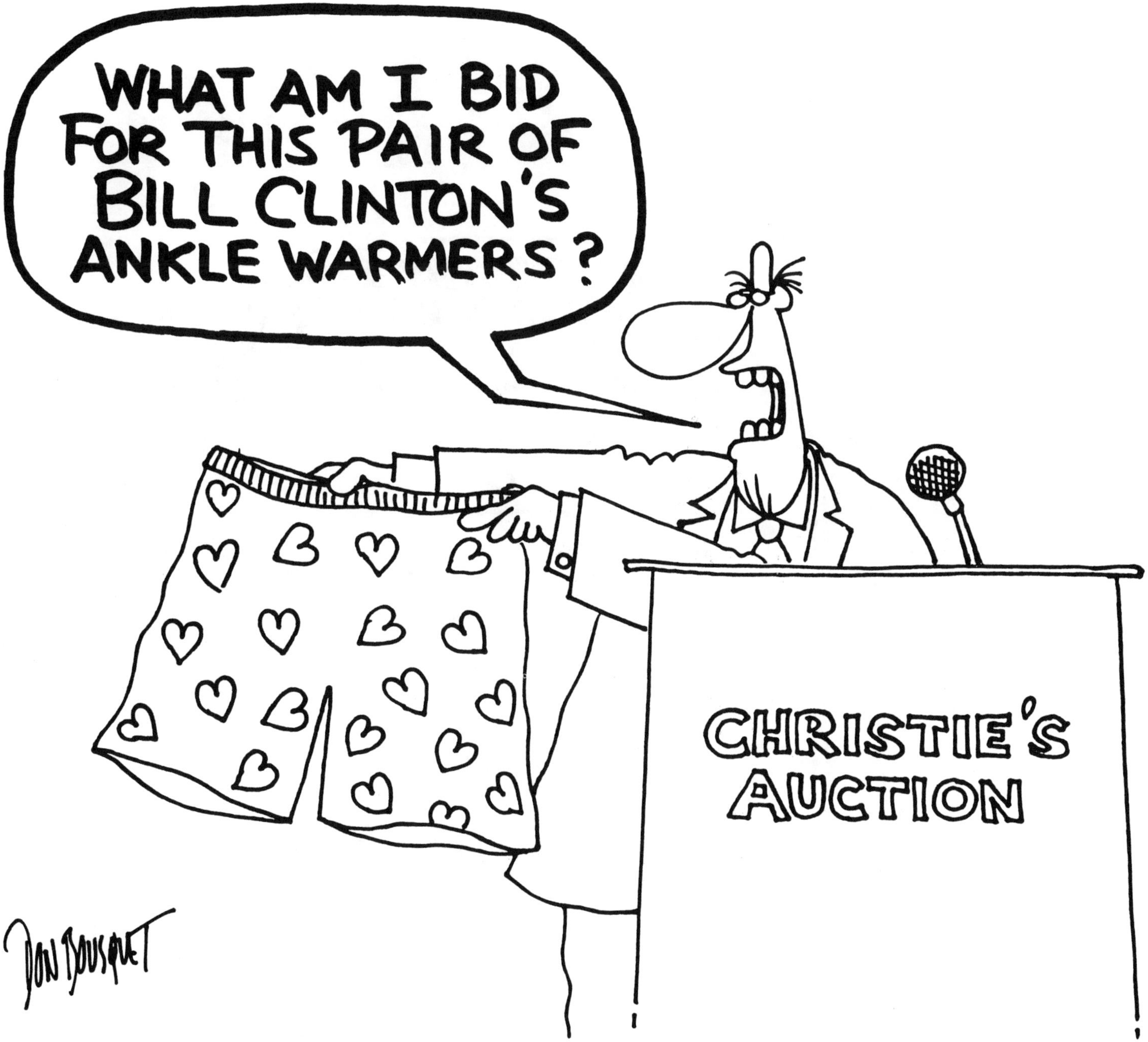
WHAT AM I BID FOR THIS PAIR OF BILL CLINTON'S ANKLE WARMERS?
CHRISTIE'S AUCTION
DON BOUSQUET

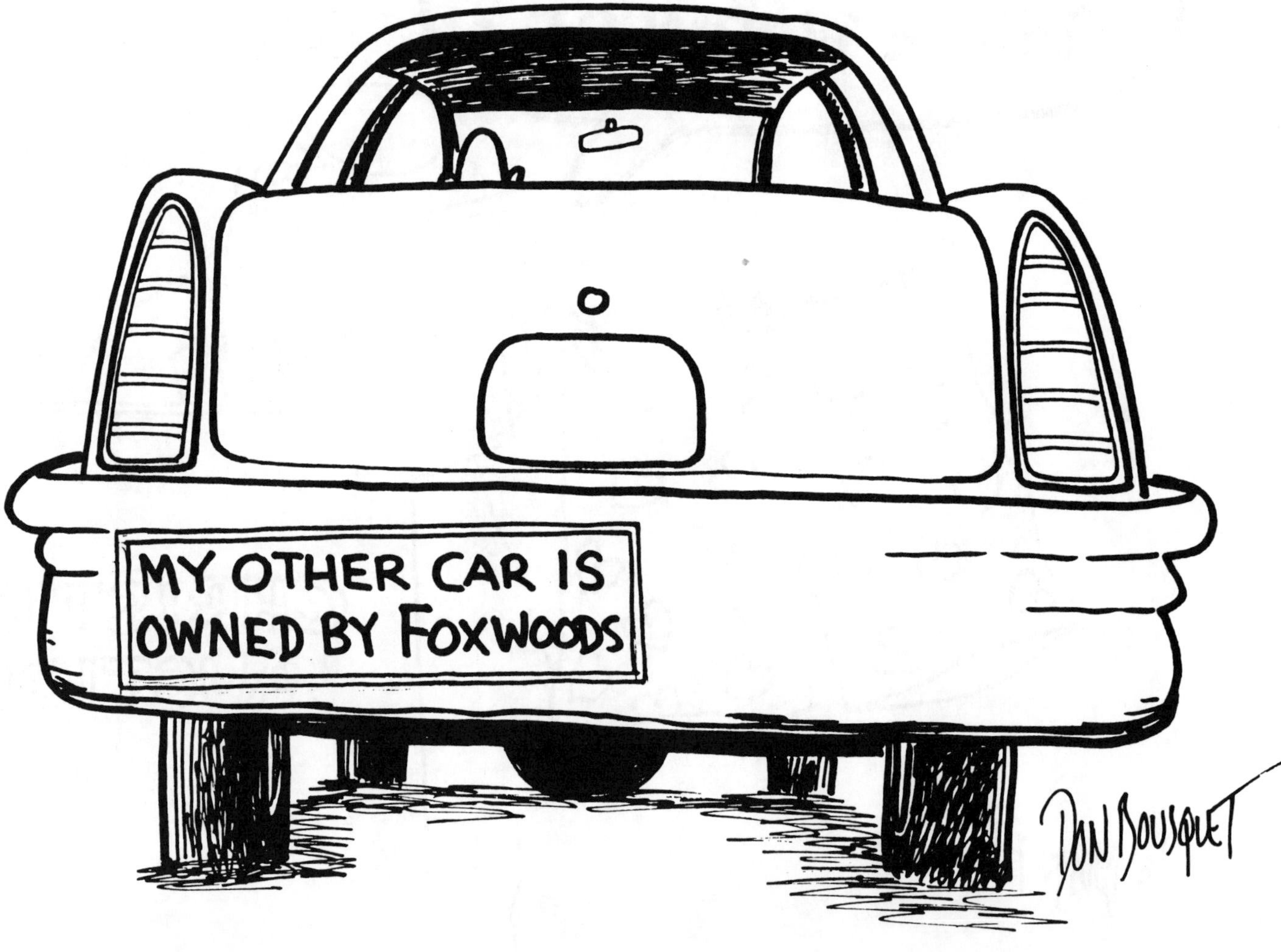
MY OTHER CAR IS
OWNED BY FOXWOODS
DON BOUSQUET

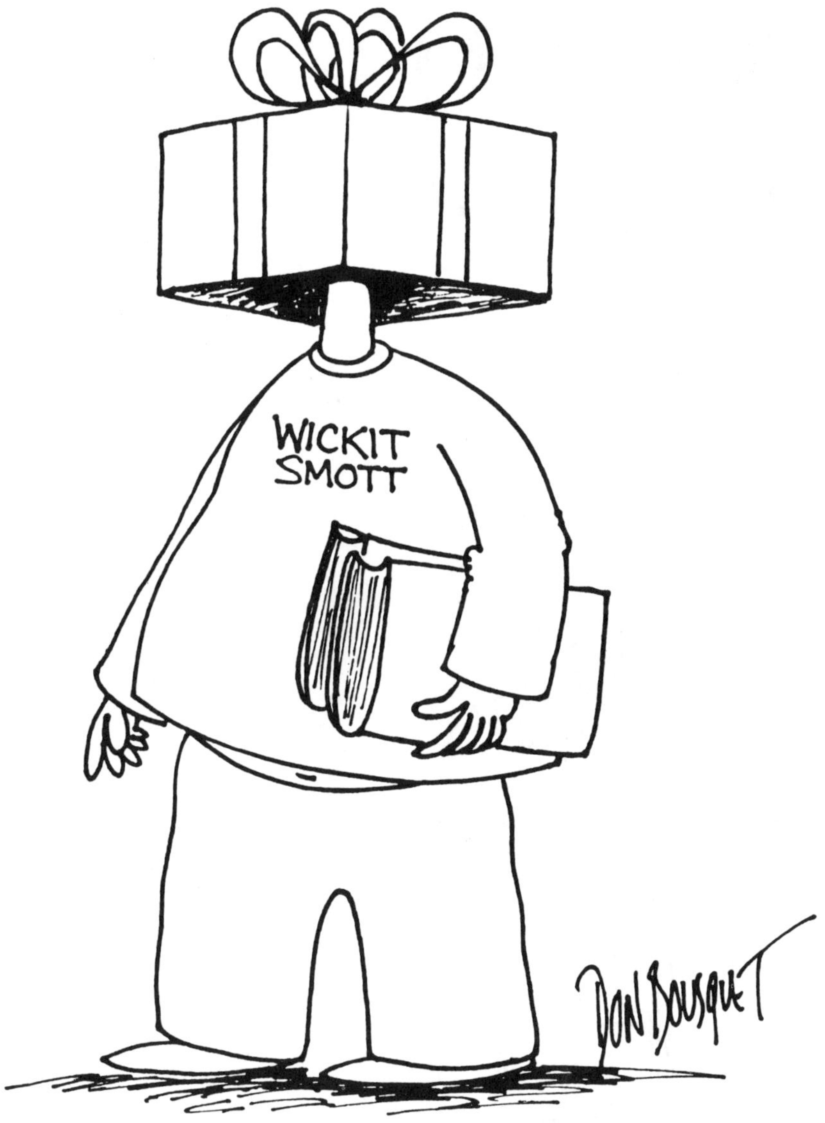
WICKIT
SMOTT
DON BOUSQUET

GIFTED CHILD

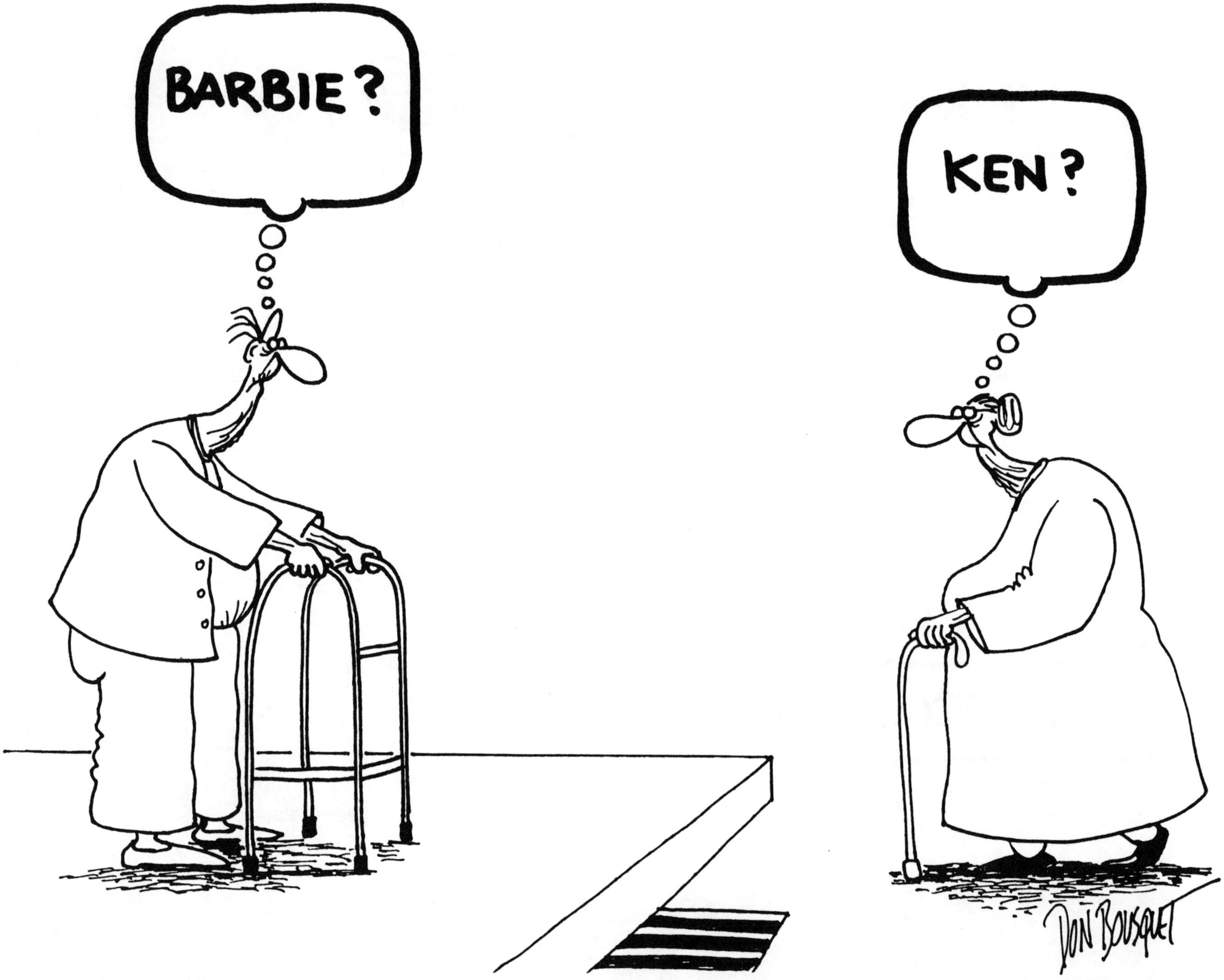
BARBIE?
KEN?
DON BOUSQUET

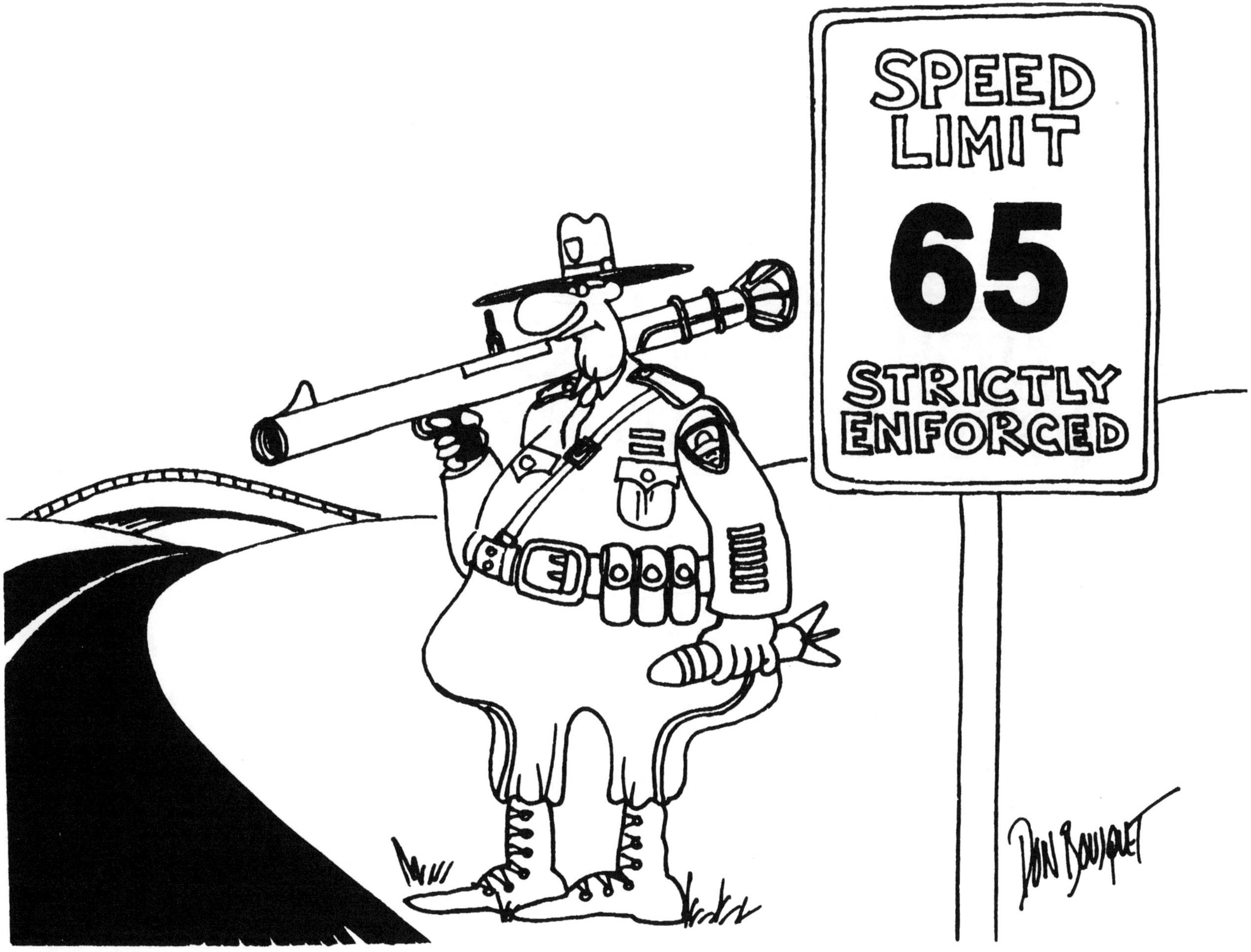
SPEED
LIMIT
65
STRICTLY
ENFORCED
DON BOUSQUET

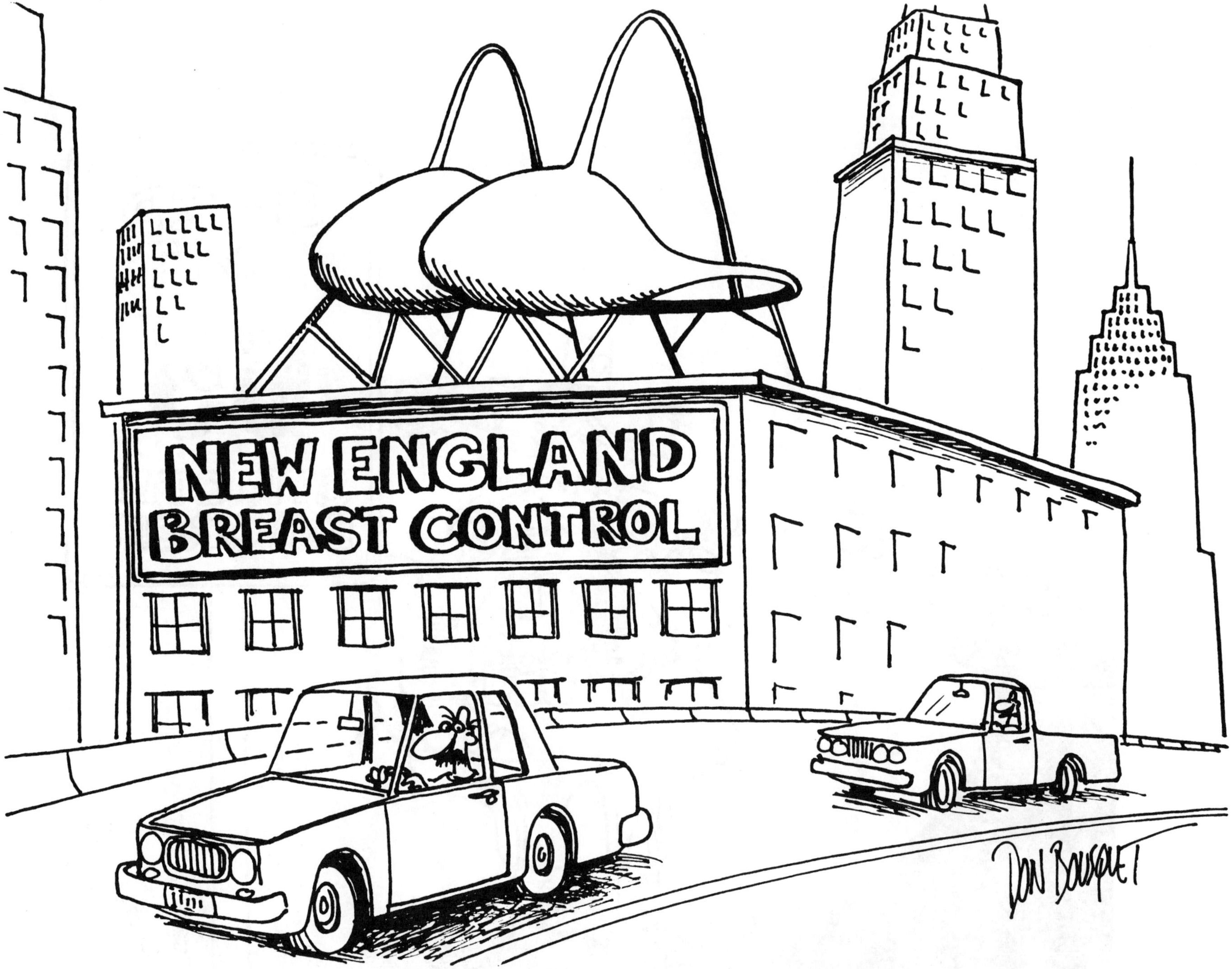
NEW ENGLAND
BREAST CONTROL
DON BOUSQUET

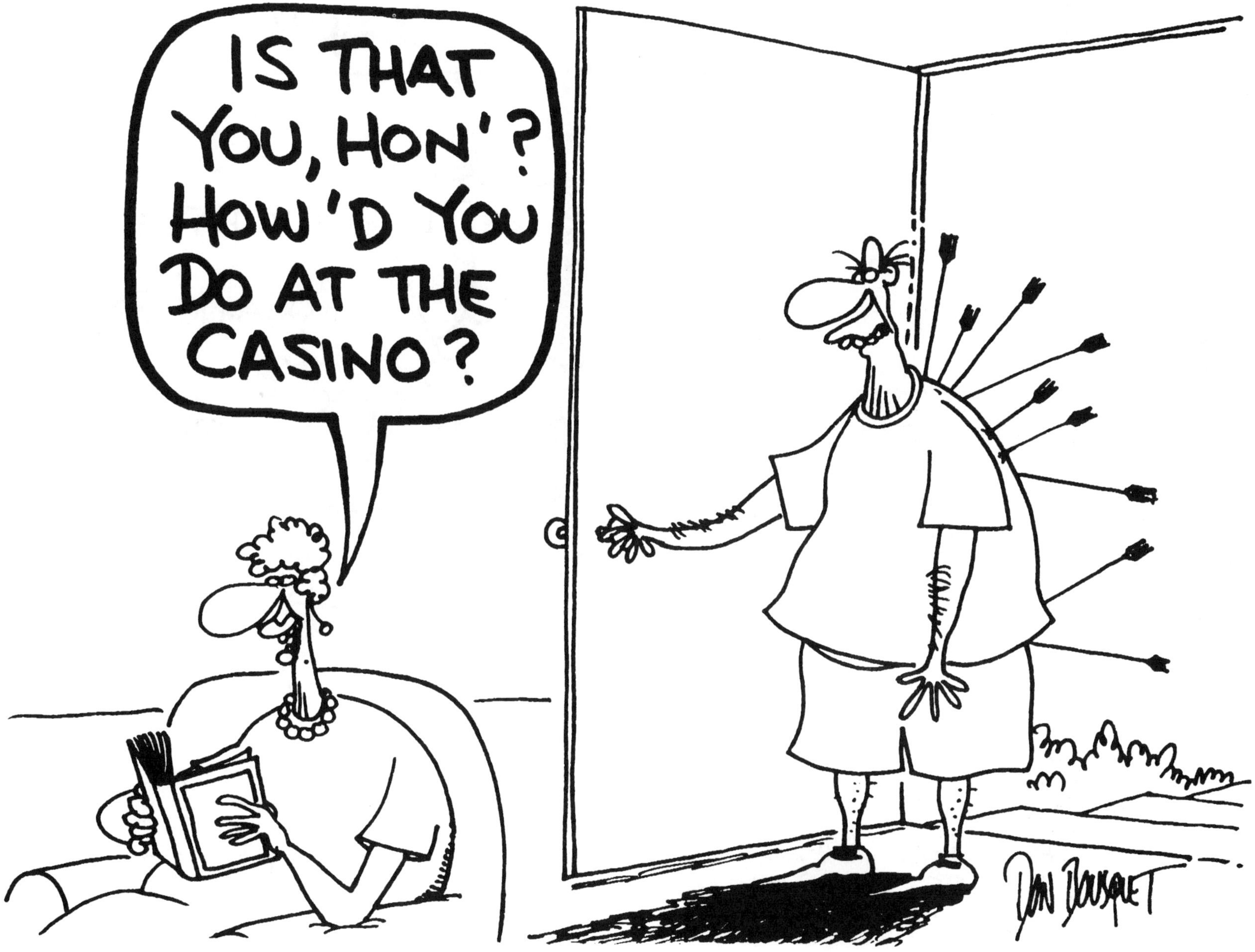
IS THAT YOU, HON'? HOW'D YOU DO AT THE CASINO?
DON BOUSQUET

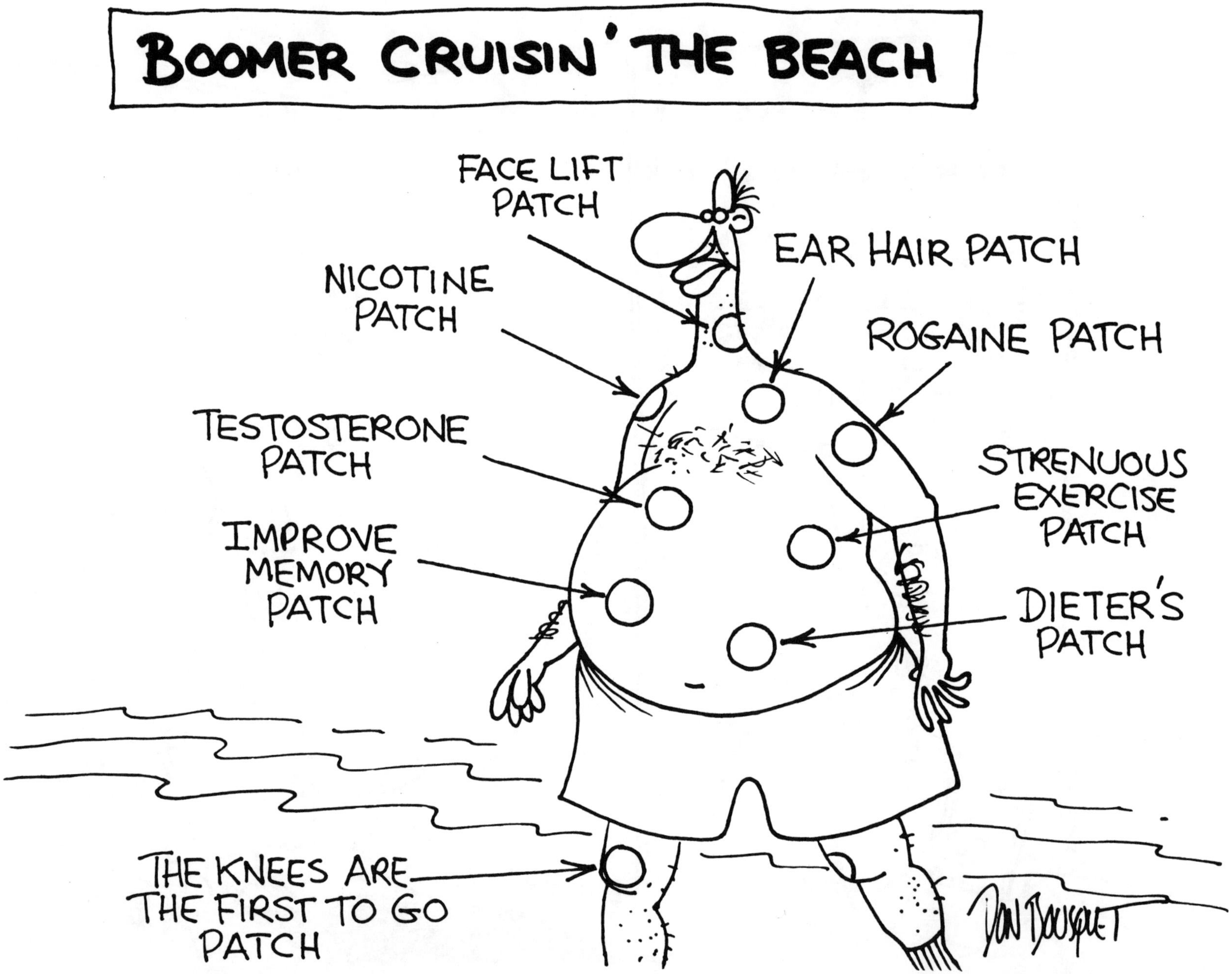
BOOMER CRUISIN' THE BEACH
FACE LIFT PATCH
NICOTINE PATCH
EAR HAIR PATCH
ROGAINE PATCH
TESTOSTERONE PATCH
STRENUOUS EXERCISE PATCH
IMPROVE MEMORY PATCH
DIETER'S PATCH
THE KNEES ARE THE FIRST TO GO PATCH
DON BOUSQUET

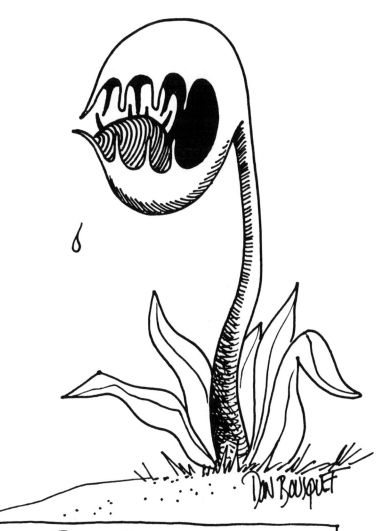

THE DEADLY
VENUS QUAHOG TRAP

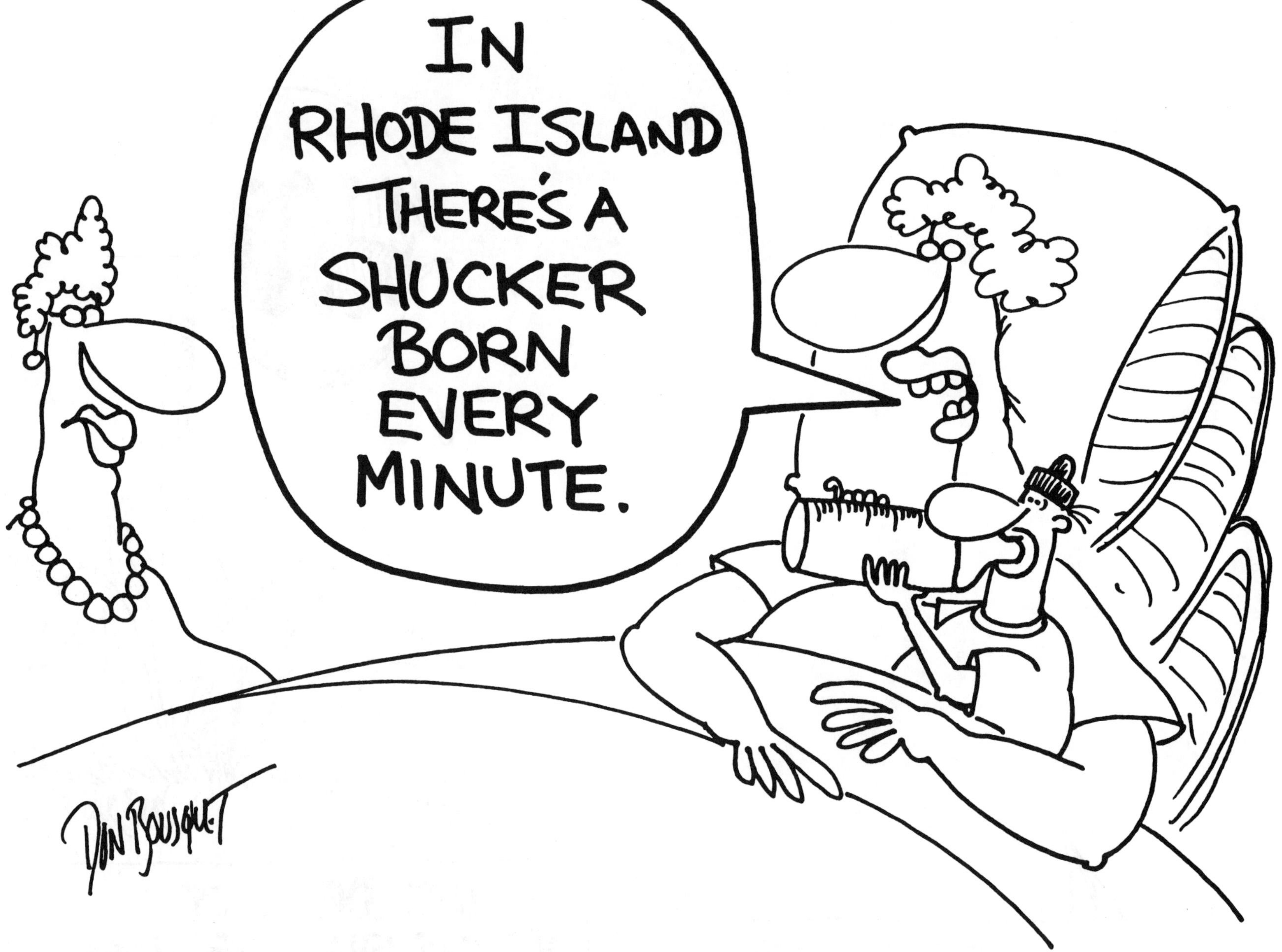
IN RHODE ISLAND THERE'S A SHUCKER BORN EVERY MINUTE.
DON BOUSQUET

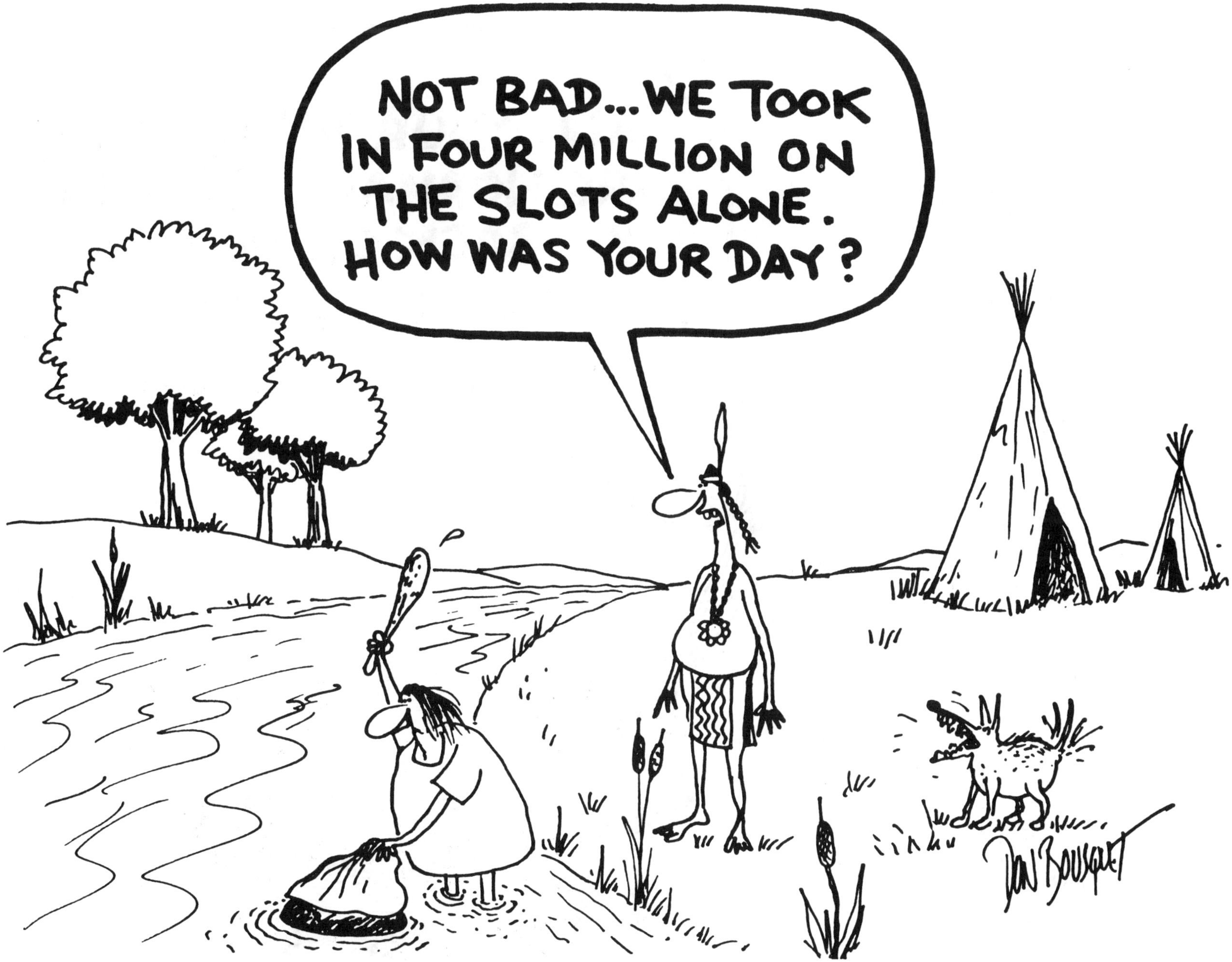
NOT BAD... WE TOOK IN FOUR MILLION ON THE SLOTS ALONE. HOW WAS YOUR DAY?
DON BOUSQUET

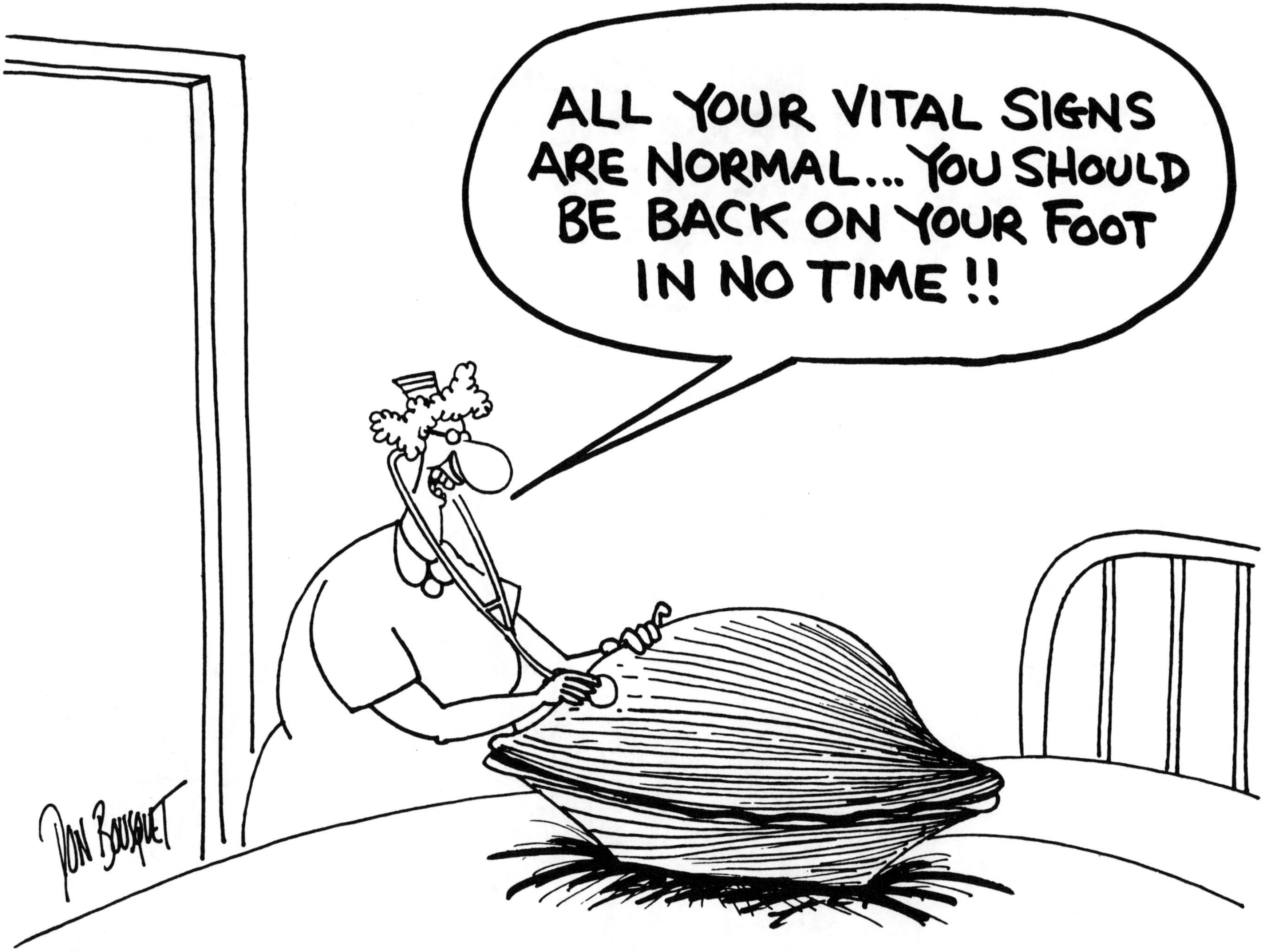
ALL YOUR VITAL SIGNS ARE NORMAL... YOU SHOULD BE BACK ON YOUR FOOT IN NO TIME !!
DON BOUSQUET

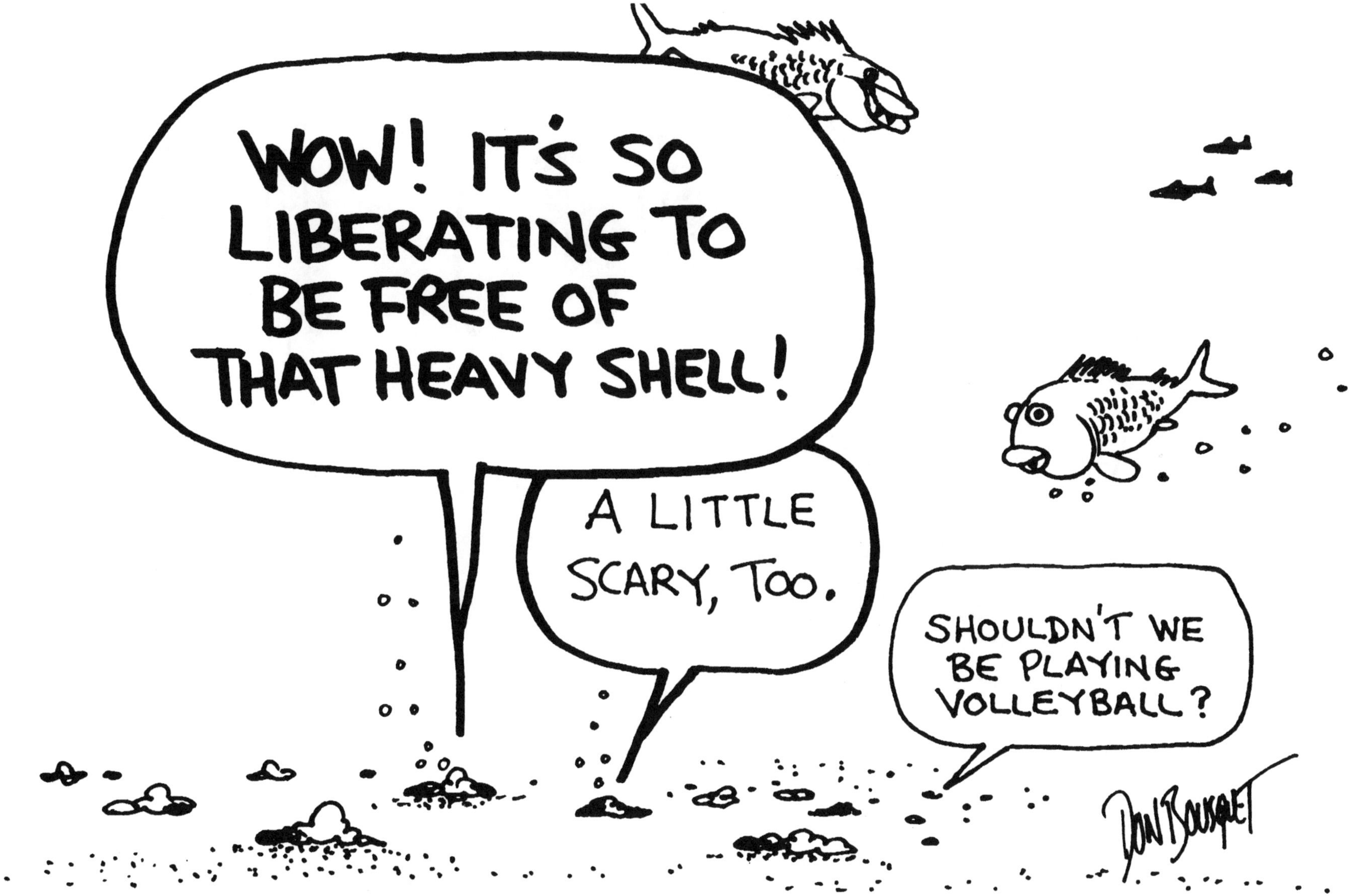
WOW! IT'S SO LIBERATING TO BE FREE OF THAT HEAVY SHELL!
A LITTLE SCARY, TOO.
SHOULDN'T WE BE PLAYING VOLLEYBALL?
DON BOUSQUET

QUAHOG NUDIST COLONY

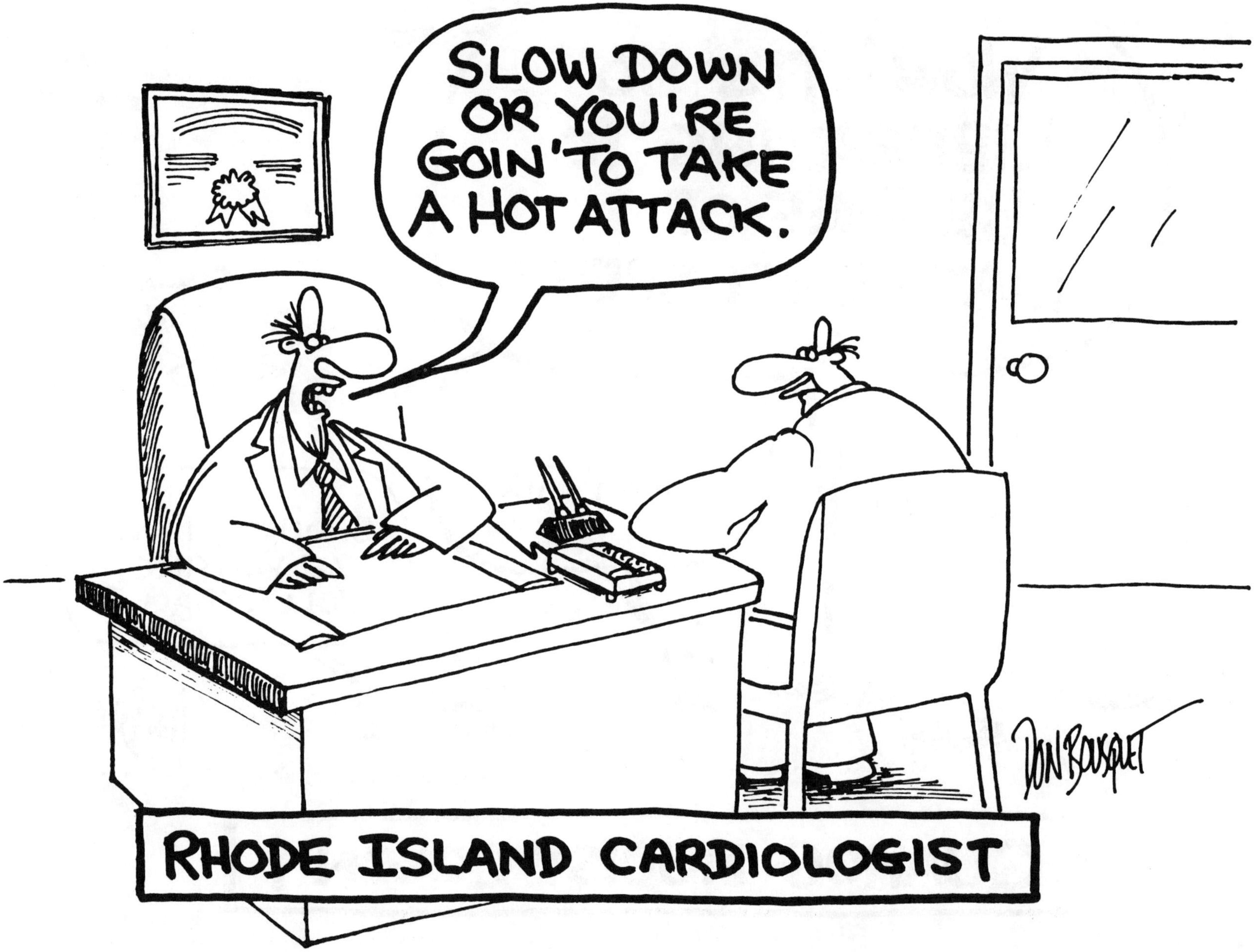
SLOW DOWN OR YOU'RE GOIN' TO TAKE A HOT ATTACK.
DON BOUSQUET
RHODE ISLAND CARDIOLOGIST

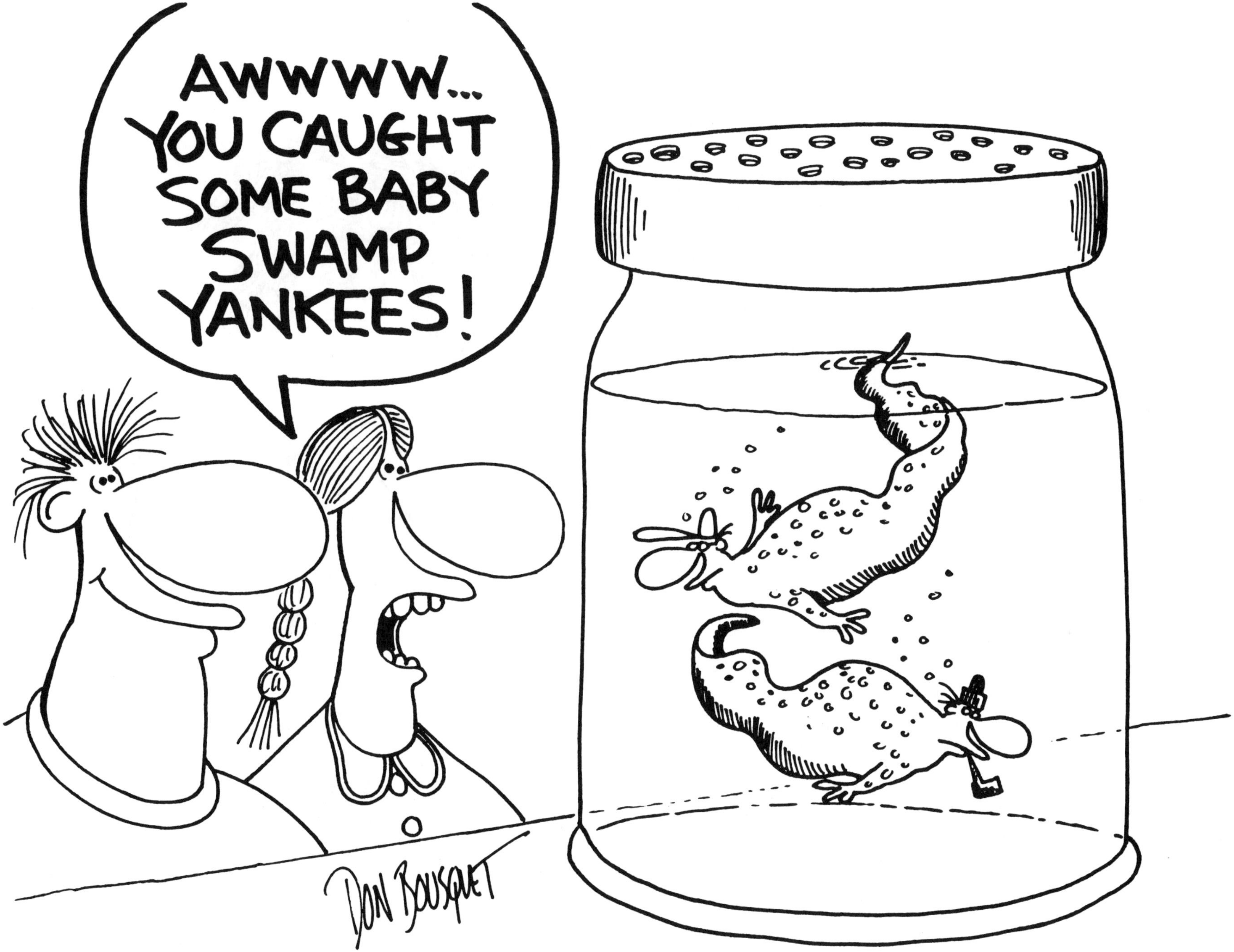
AWWWW... YOU CAUGHT SOME BABY SWAMP YANKEES!
DON BOUSQUET

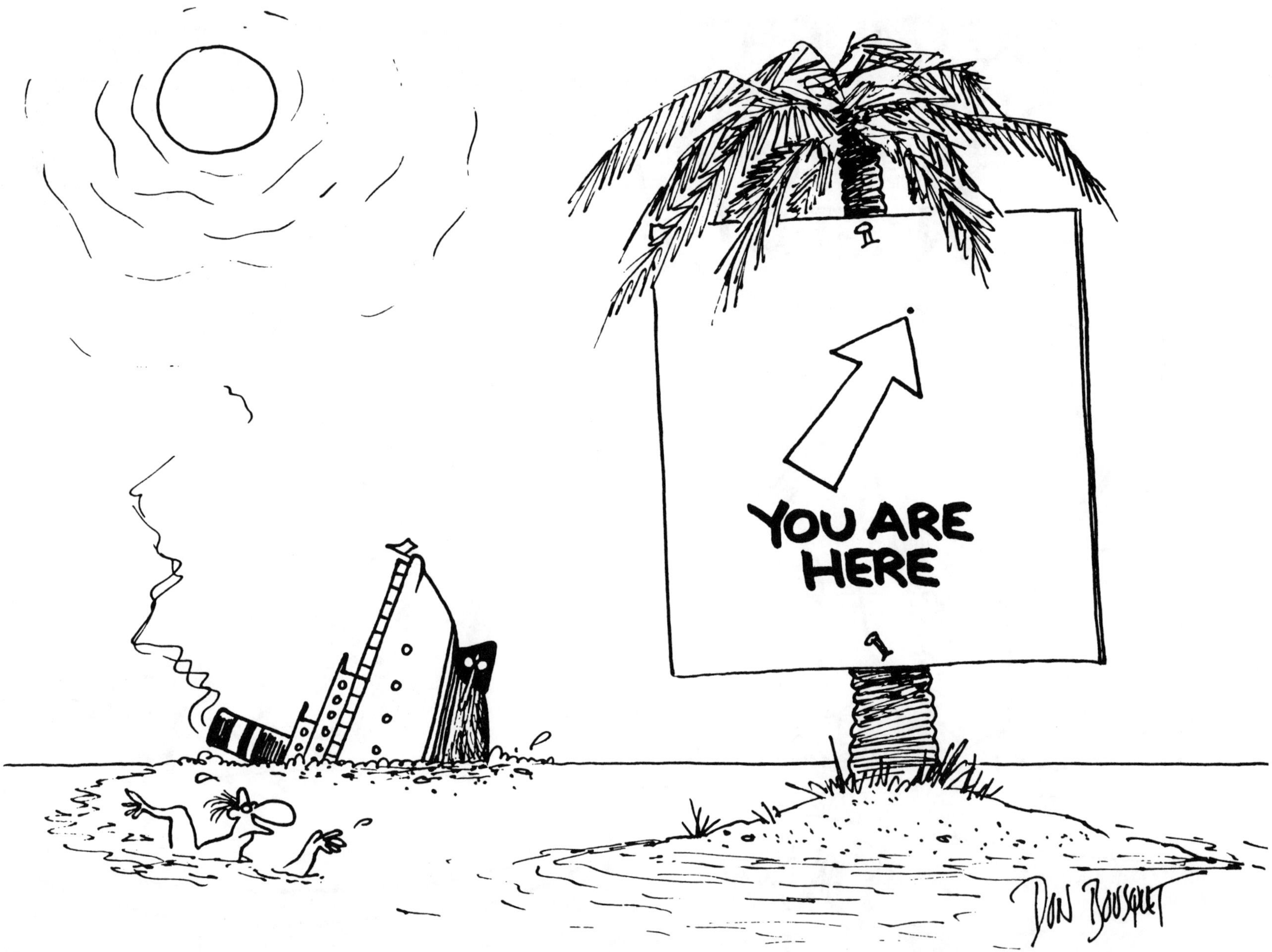
YOU ARE HERE
DON BOUSQUET

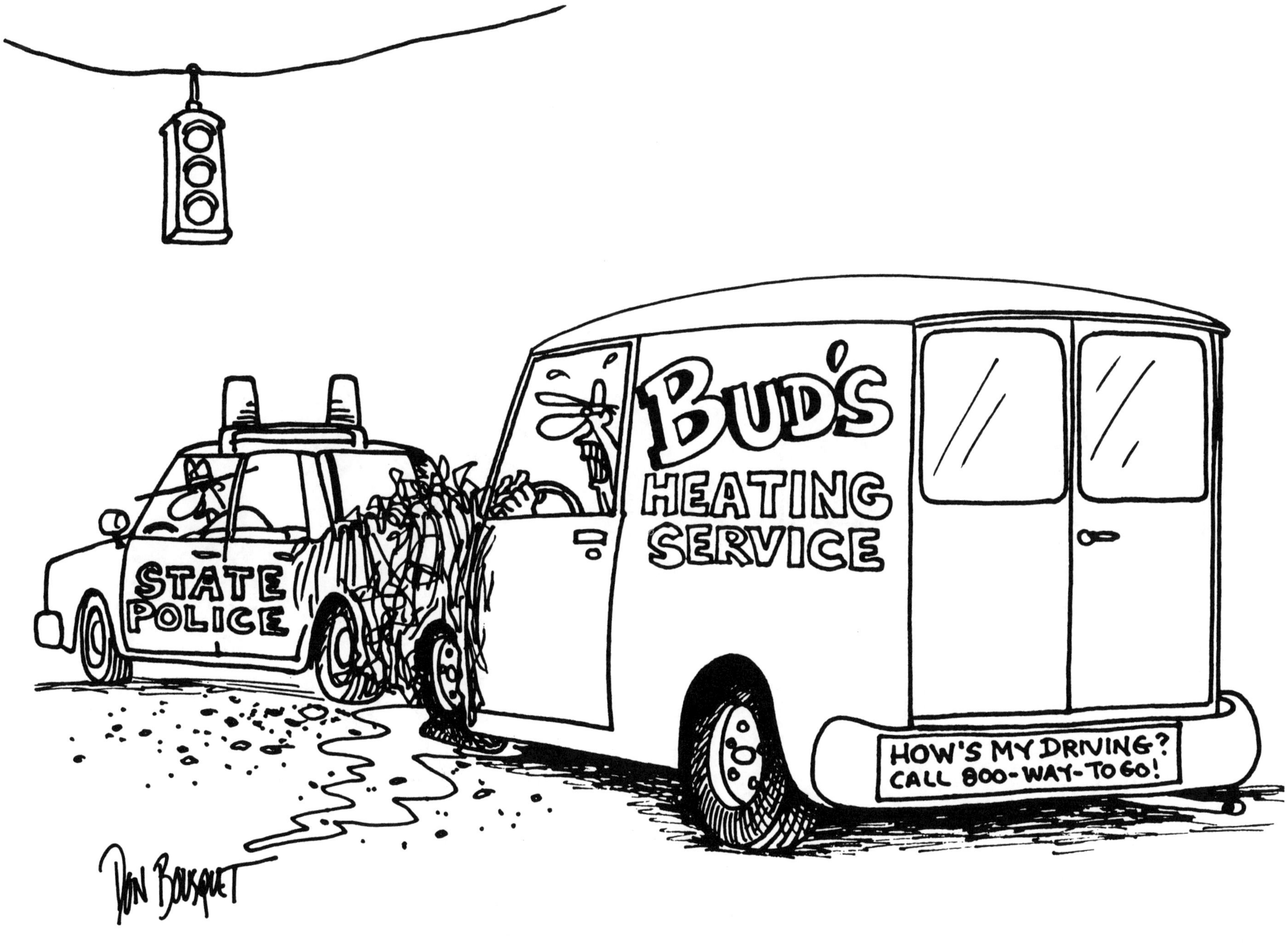
STATE
POLICE
BUD'S
HEATING
SERVICE
HOW'S MY DRIVING?
CALL 800-WAY-TO GO!
DON BOUSQUET

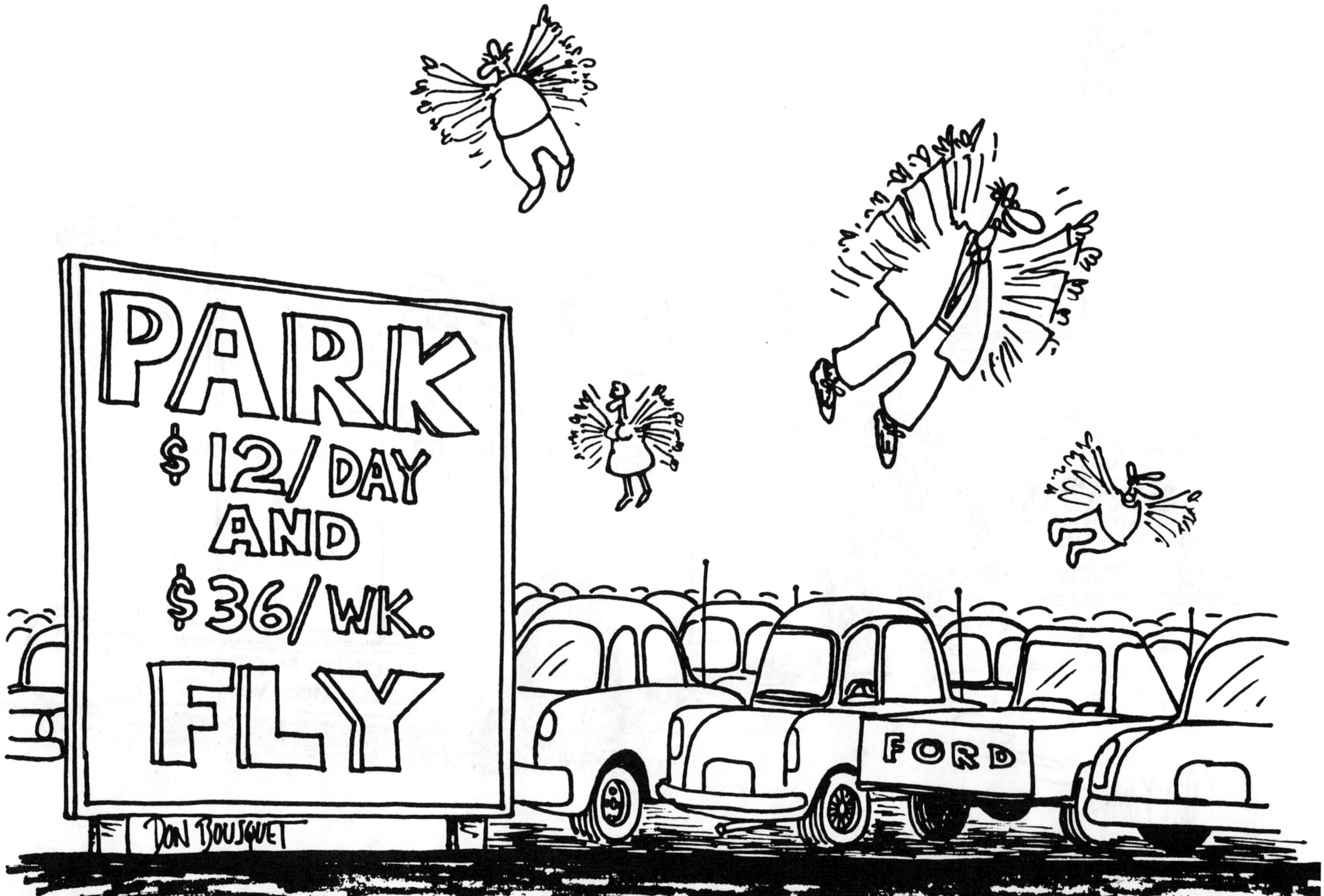
PARK
$12/DAY
AND
$36/WK.
FLY
FORD
DON BOUSQUET

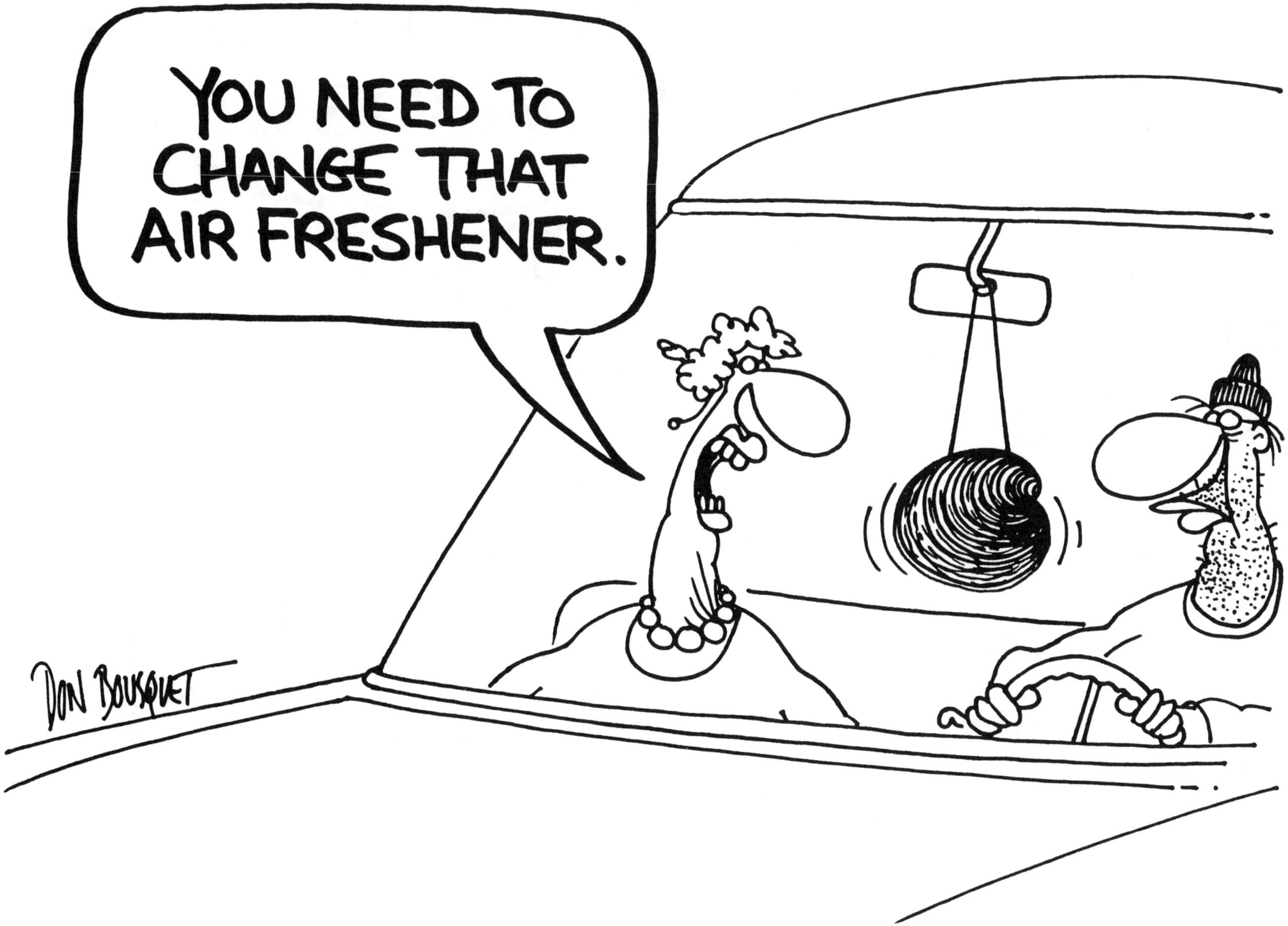
YOU NEED TO CHANGE THAT AIR FRESHENER.
DON BOUSQUET

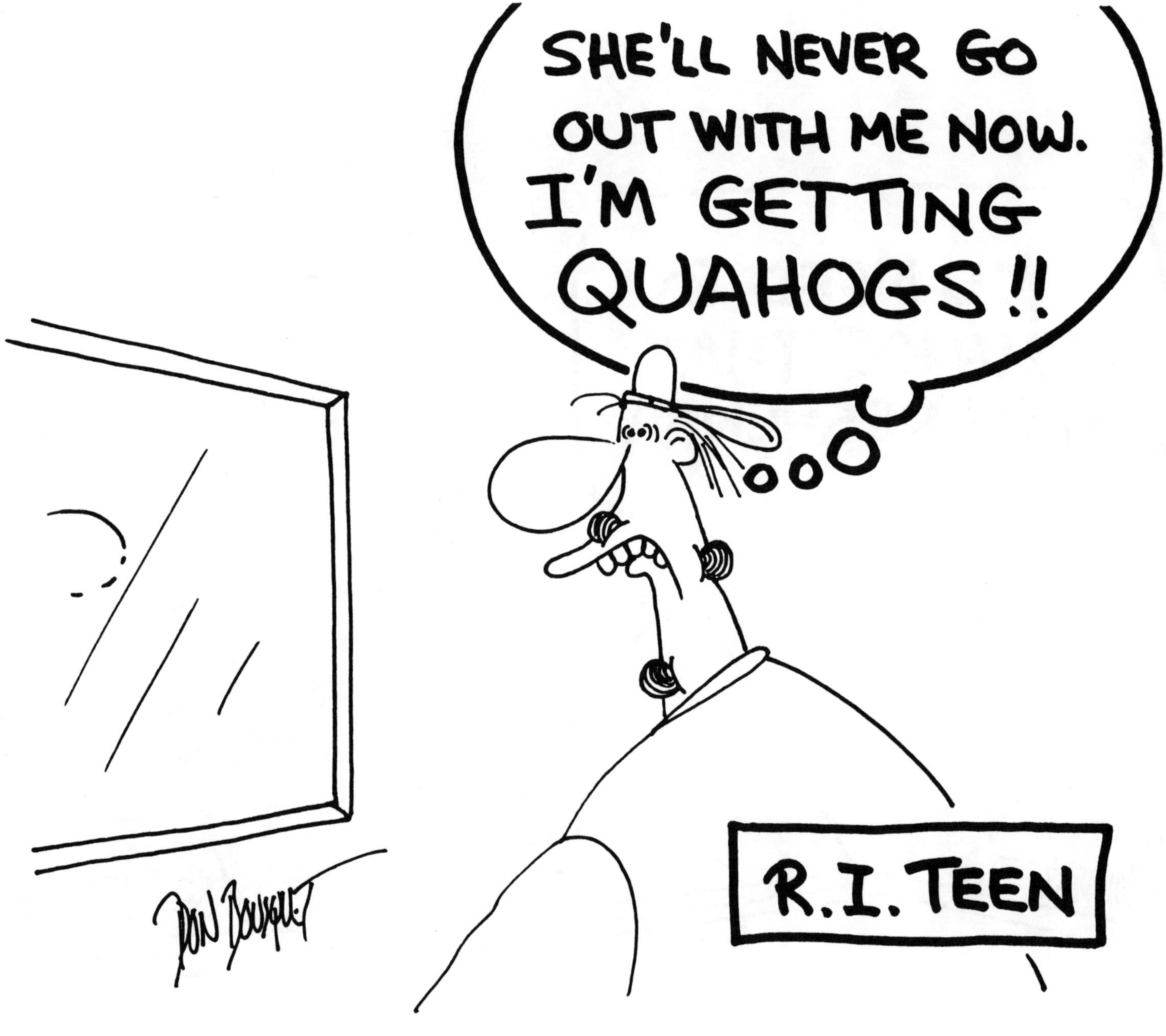
SHE'LL NEVER GO OUT WITH ME NOW. I'M GETTING QUAHOGS!!
R.I. TEEN
DON BOUSQUET

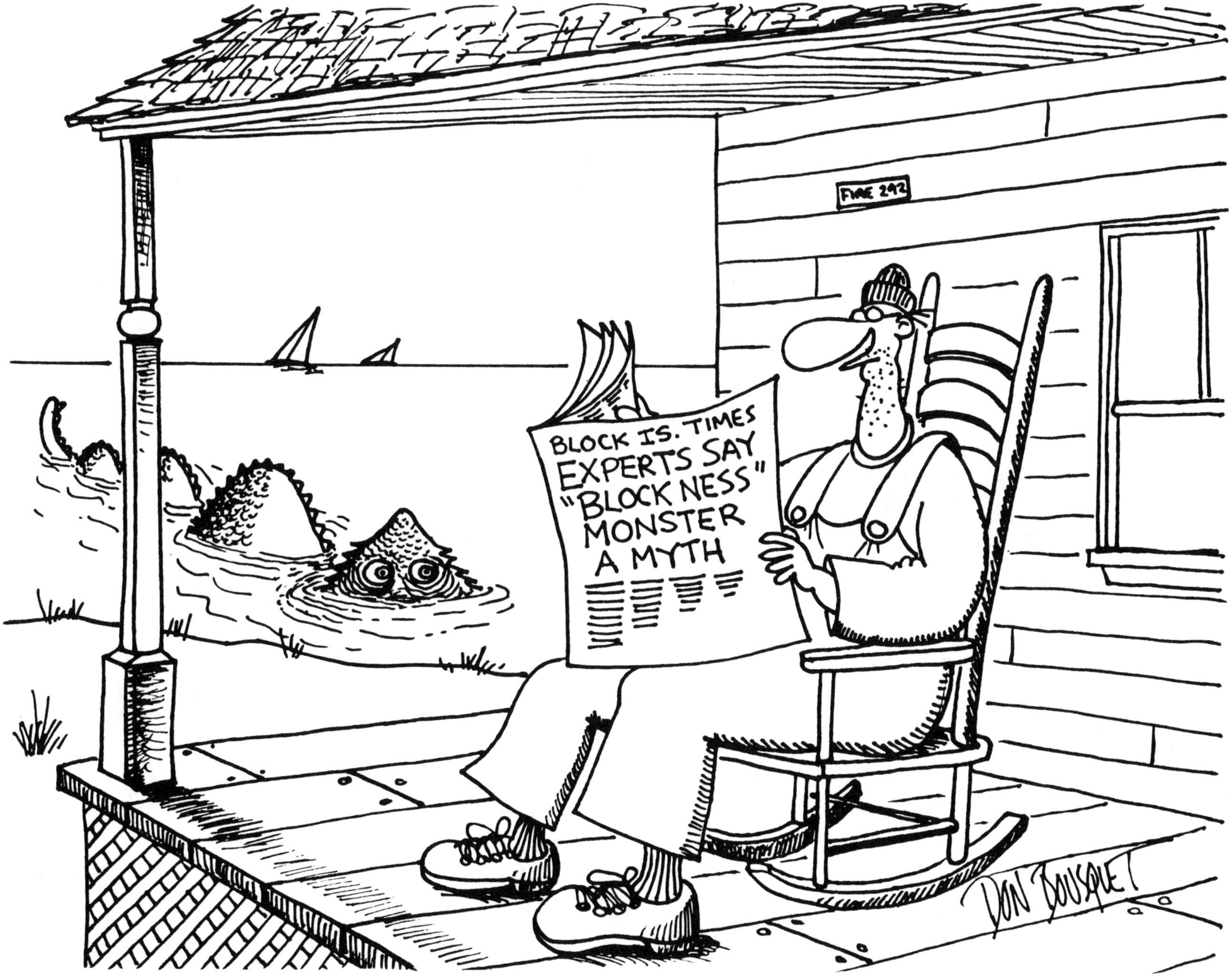
FIRE 292
BLOCK IS. TIMES
EXPERTS SAY
"BLOCK NESS"
MONSTER
A MYTH
DON BOUSQUET

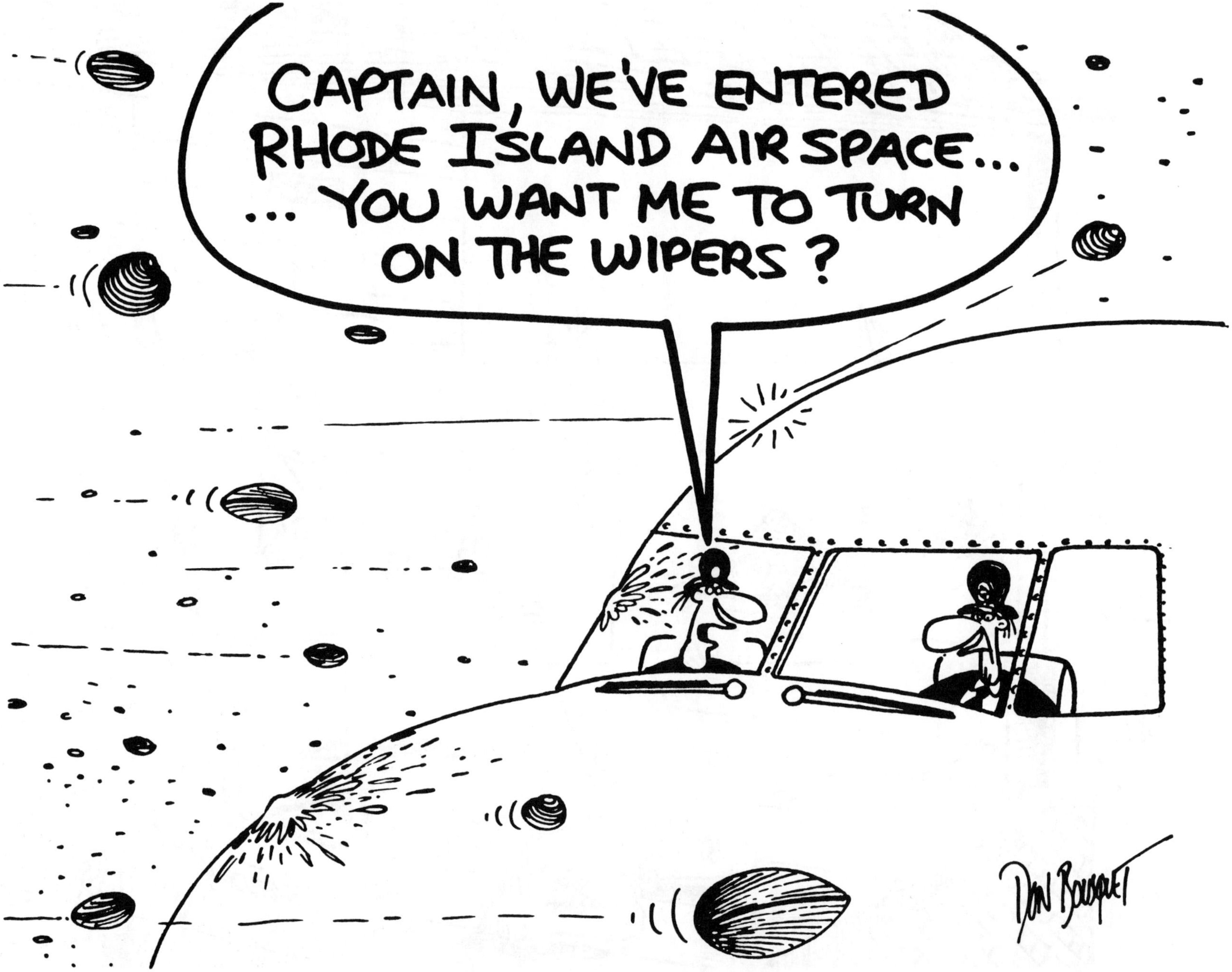
CAPTAIN, WE'VE ENTERED RHODE ISLAND AIR SPACE... ...YOU WANT ME TO TURN ON THE WIPERS?
DON BOUSQUET

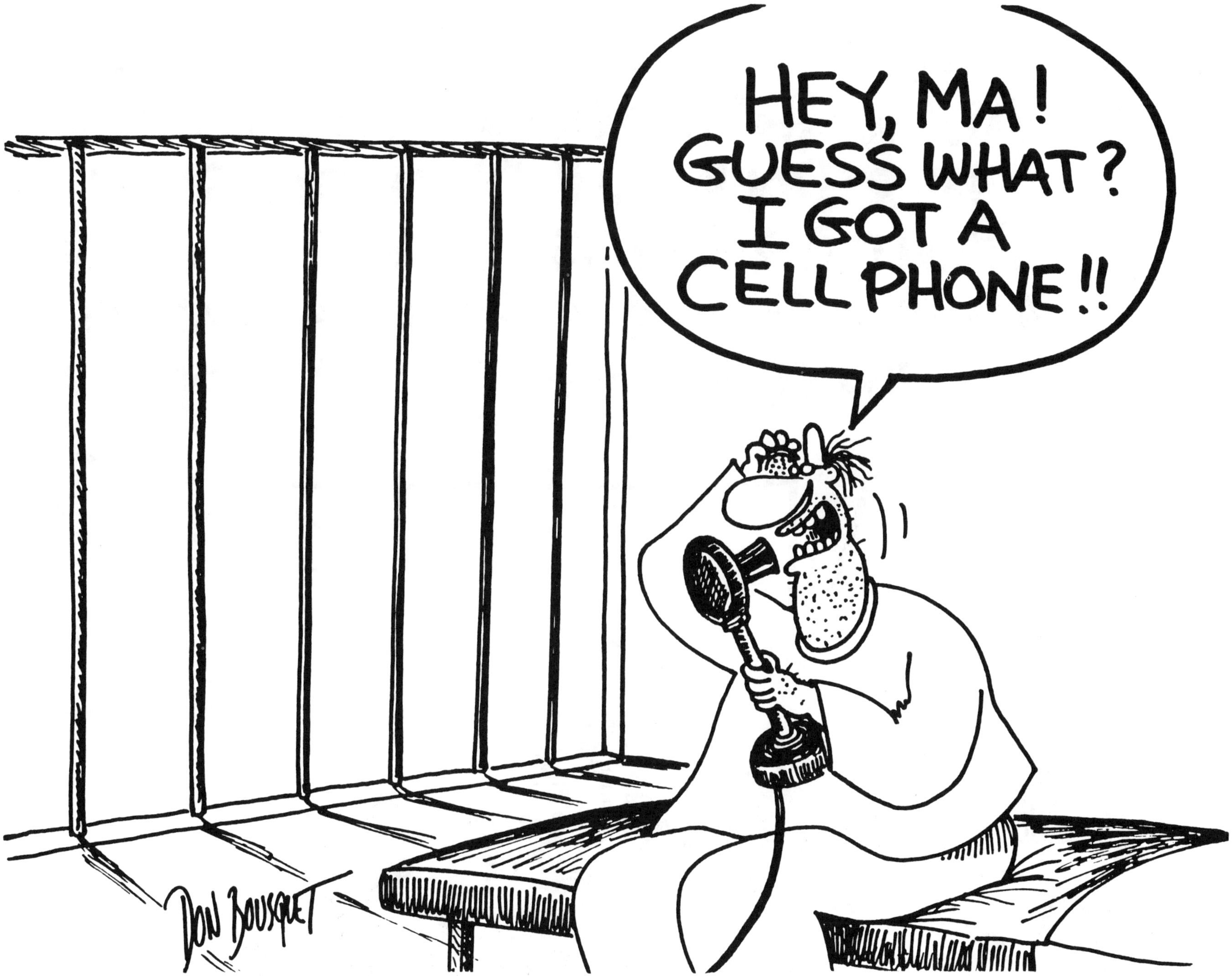
HEY, MA!
GUESS WHAT?
I GOT A
CELL PHONE!!
DON BOUSQUET

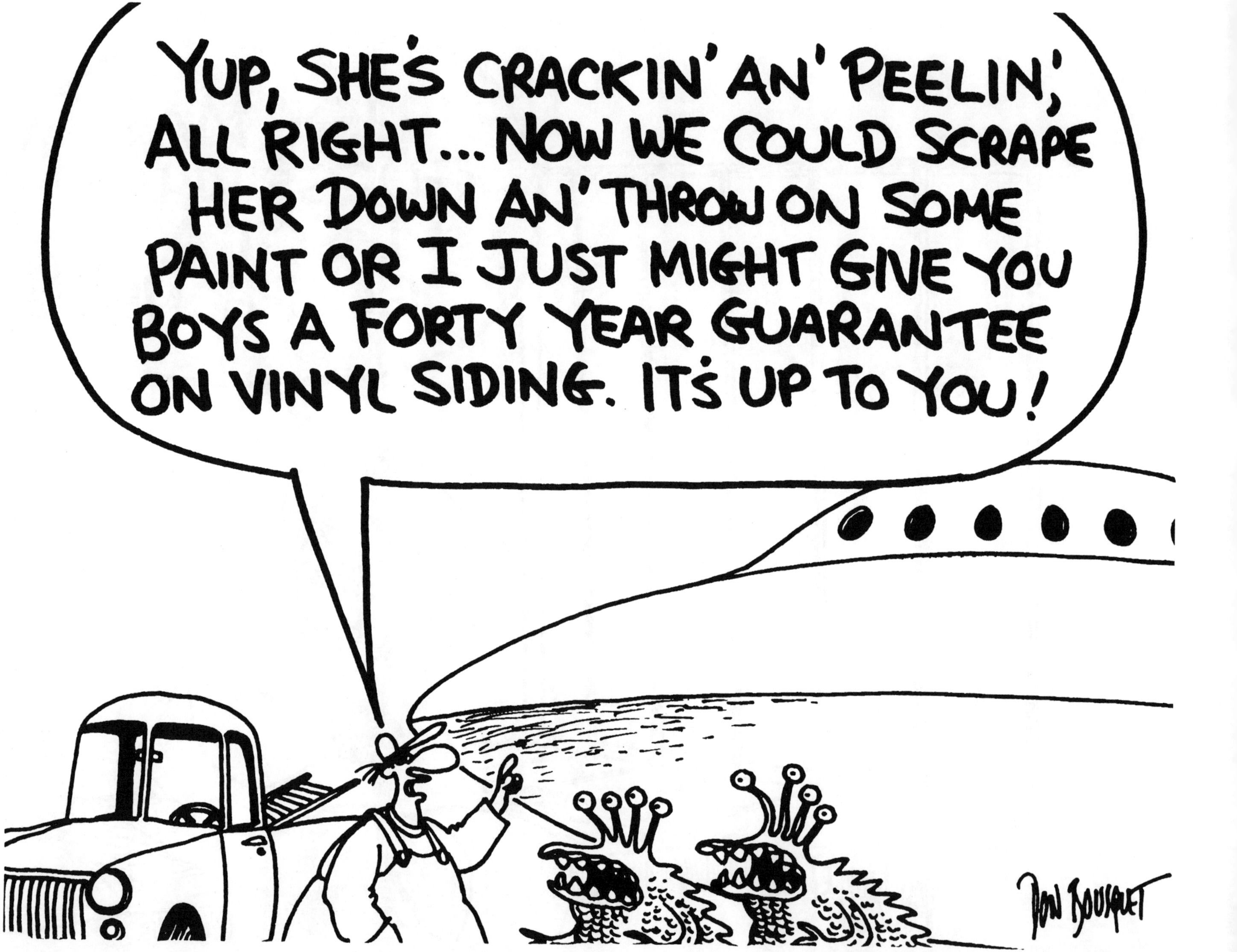
YUP, SHE'S CRACKIN' AN' PEELIN', ALL RIGHT... NOW WE COULD SCRAPE HER DOWN AN' THROW ON SOME PAINT OR I JUST MIGHT GIVE YOU BOYS A FORTY YEAR GUARANTEE ON VINYL SIDING. IT'S UP TO YOU!
DON BOUSQUET

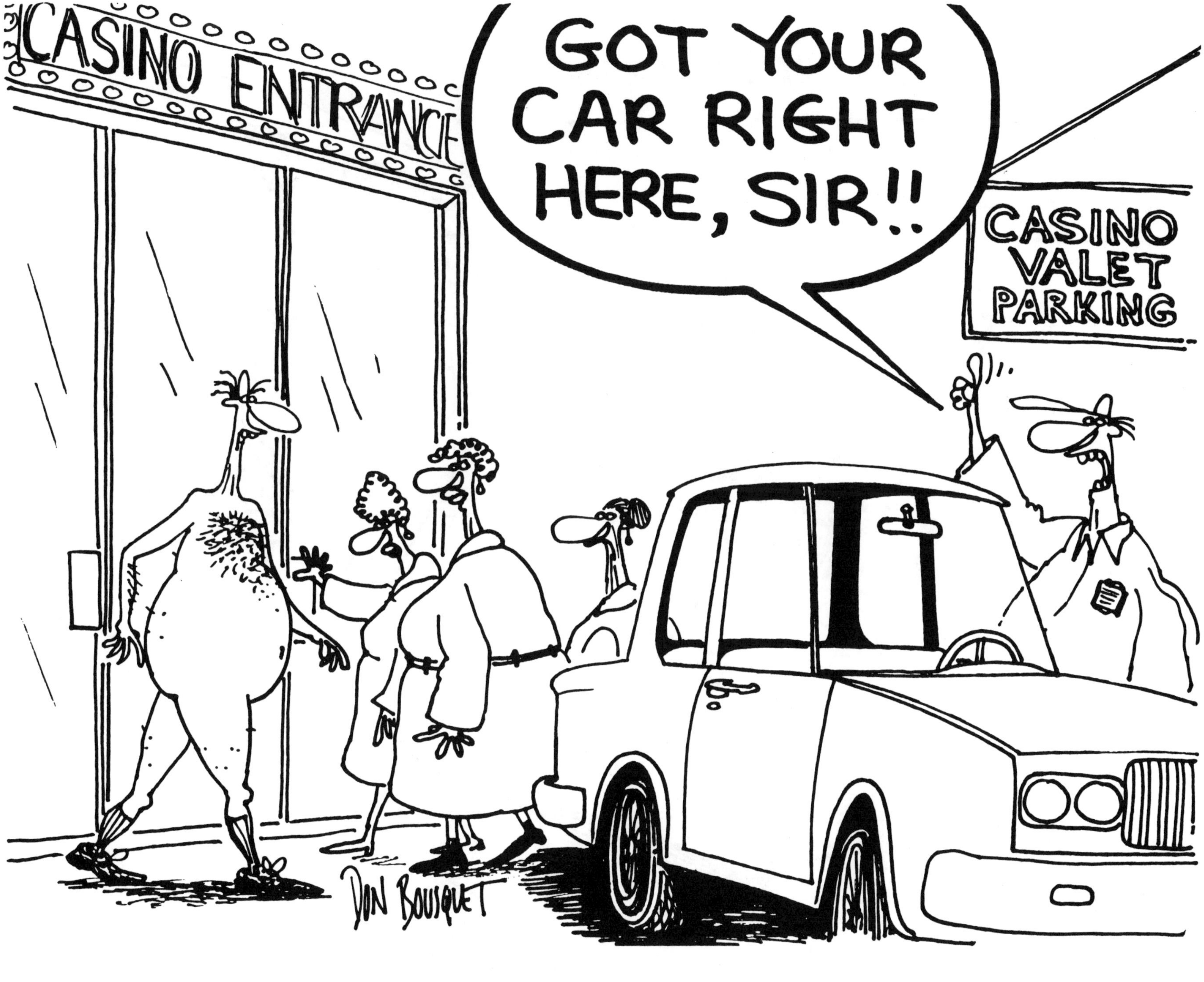
CASINO ENTRANCE
GOT YOUR CAR RIGHT HERE, SIR!!
CASINO VALET PARKING
DON BOUSQUET

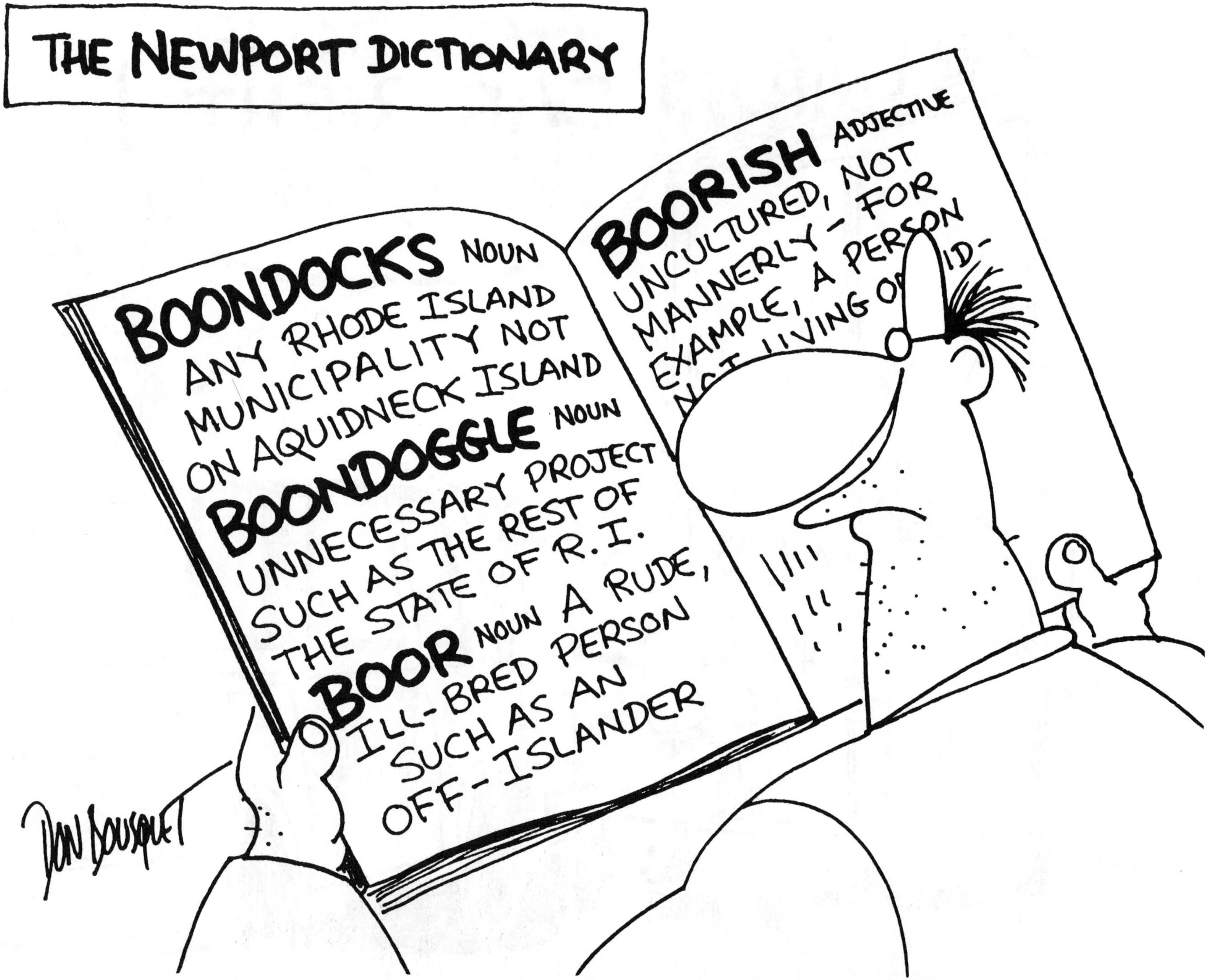
THE NEWPORT DICTIONARY
BOONDOCKS NOUN
ANY RHODE ISLAND MUNICIPALITY NOT ON AQUIDNECK ISLAND
BOONDOGGLE NOUN
UNNECESSARY PROJECT SUCH AS THE REST OF THE STATE OF R.I.
BOOR NOUN A RUDE, ILL-BRED PERSON SUCH AS AN OFF-ISLANDER
BOORISH ADJECTIVE
UNCULTURED, NOT MANNERLY - FOR EXAMPLE, A PERSON
DON BOUSQUET

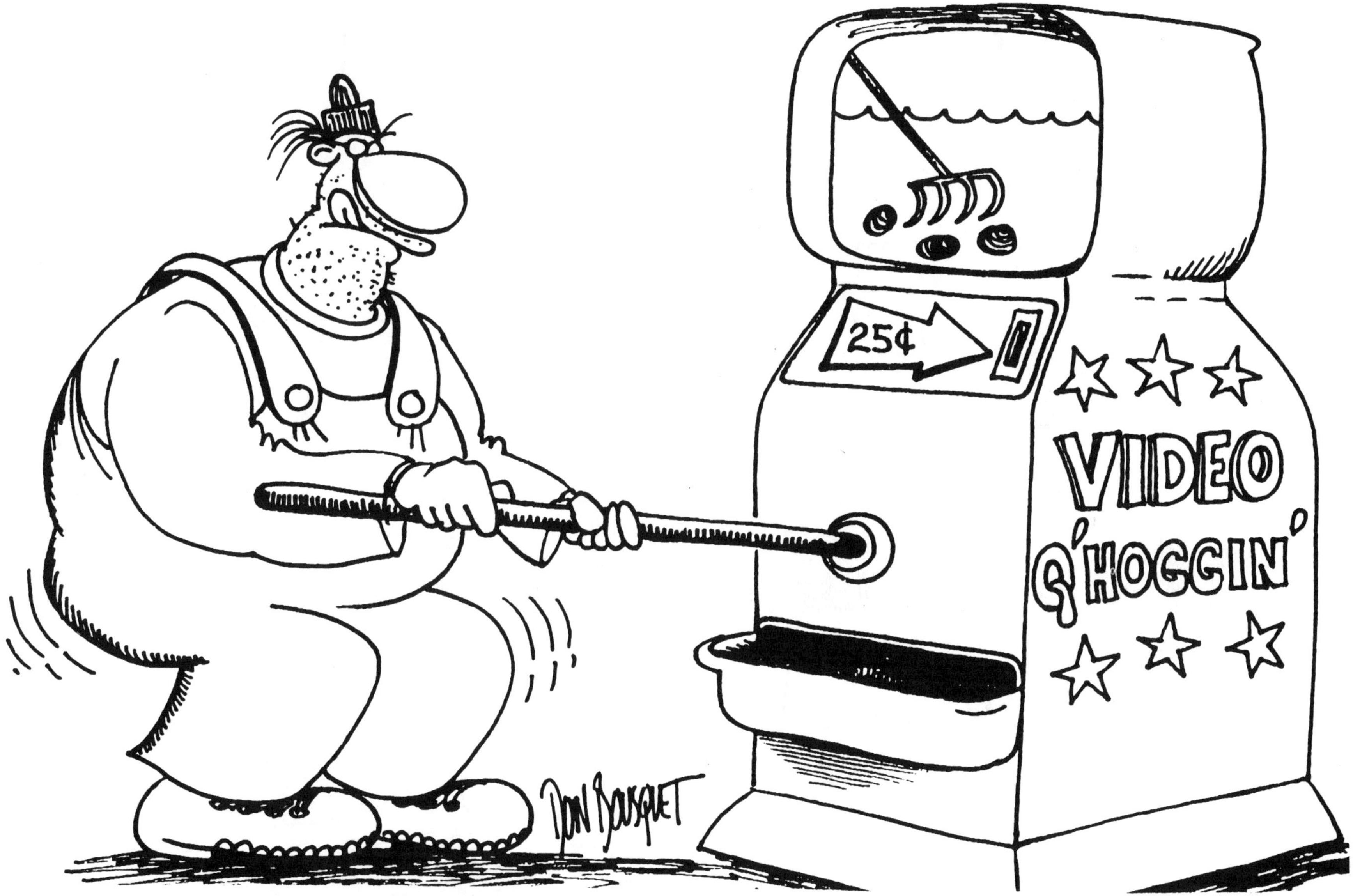

25¢
VIDEO
O'HOGGIN'
DON BOUSQUET

THAT ONE BELONGS TO MY DOCTOR... IT STANDS FOR, "BETTER ORDER ANOTHER TEST."

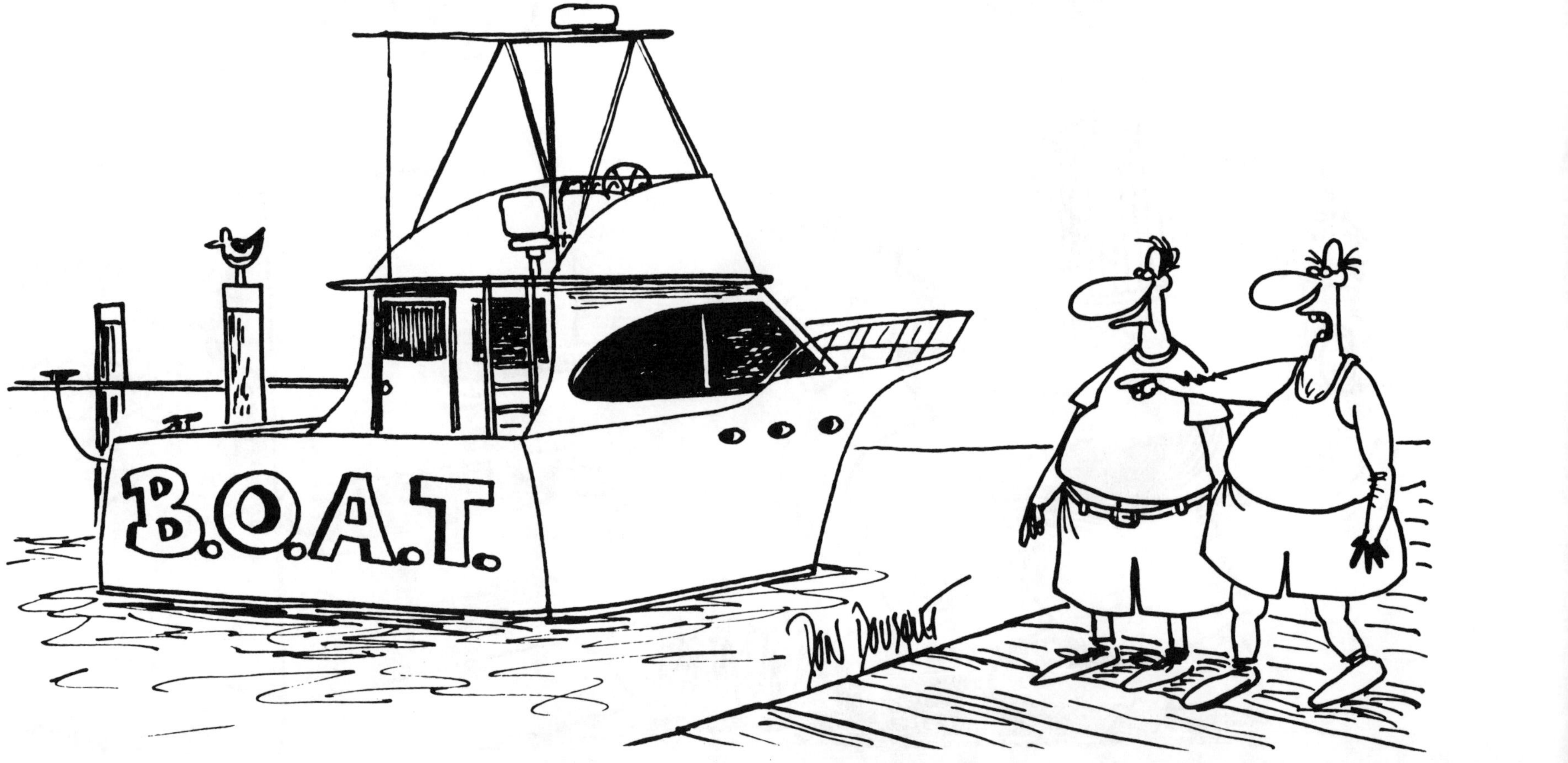
B.O.A.T.

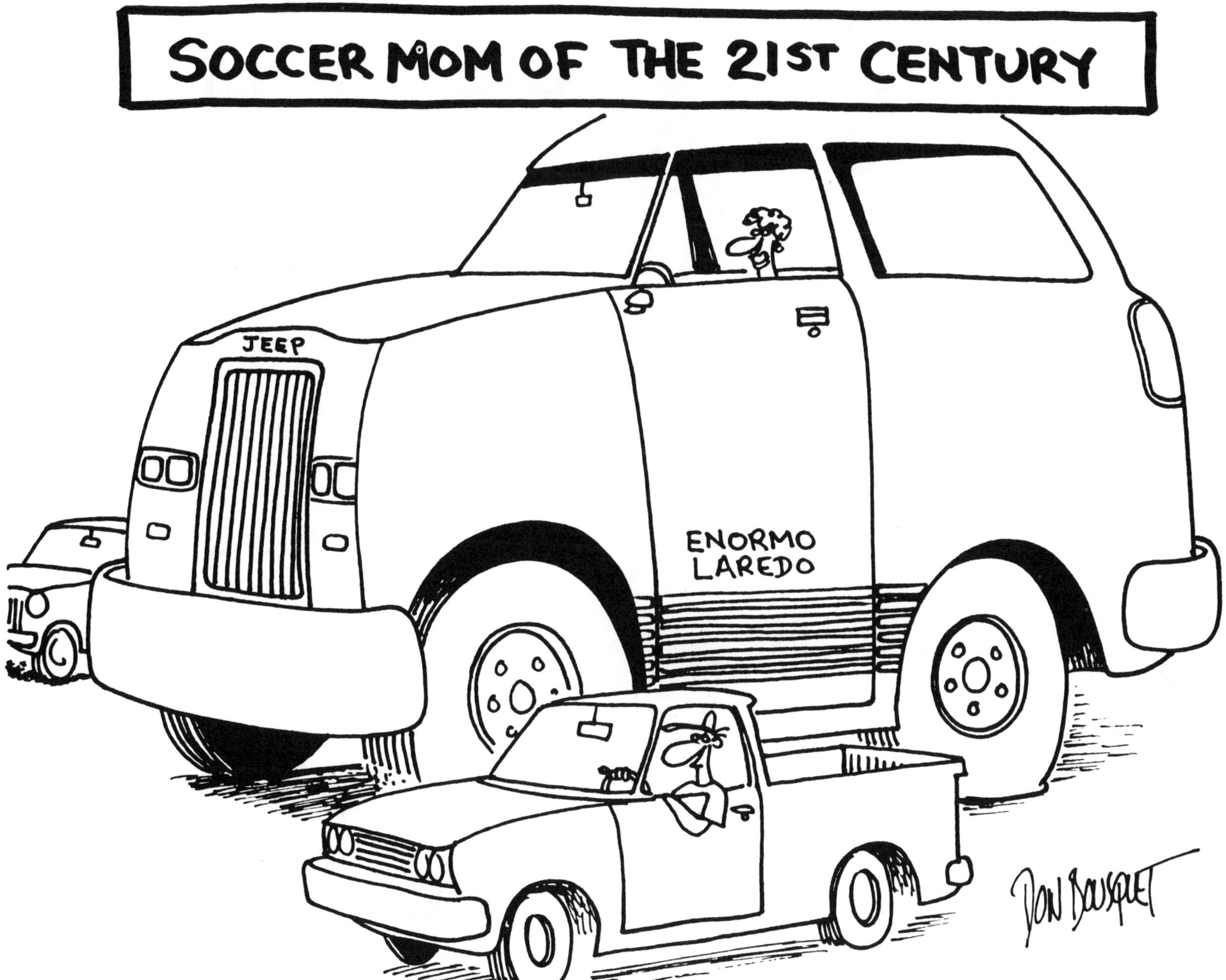
SOCCER MOM OF THE 21ST CENTURY
JEEP
ENORMO
LAREDO
DON BOUSQUET

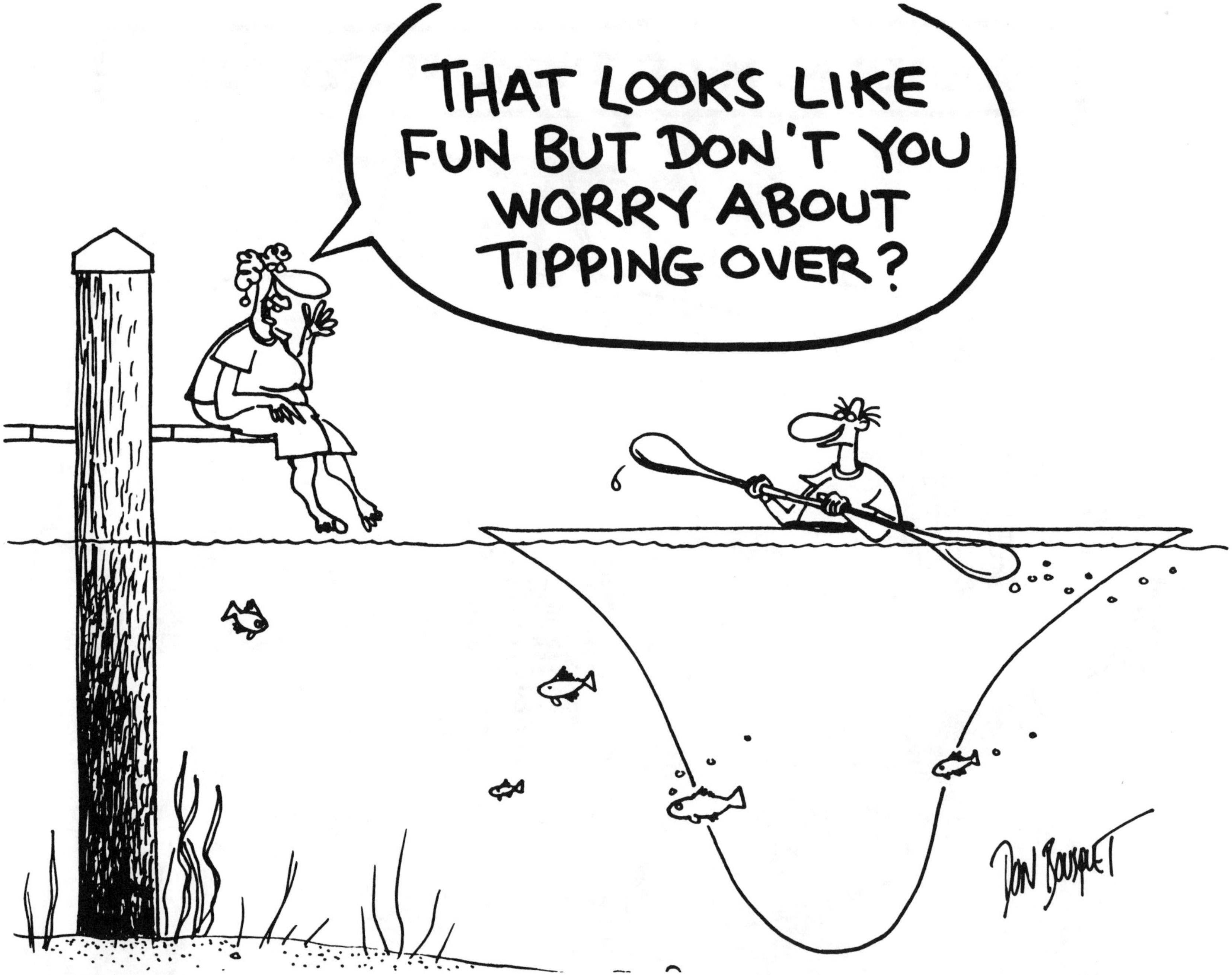
THAT LOOKS LIKE FUN BUT DON'T YOU WORRY ABOUT TIPPING OVER?
DON BOUSQUET

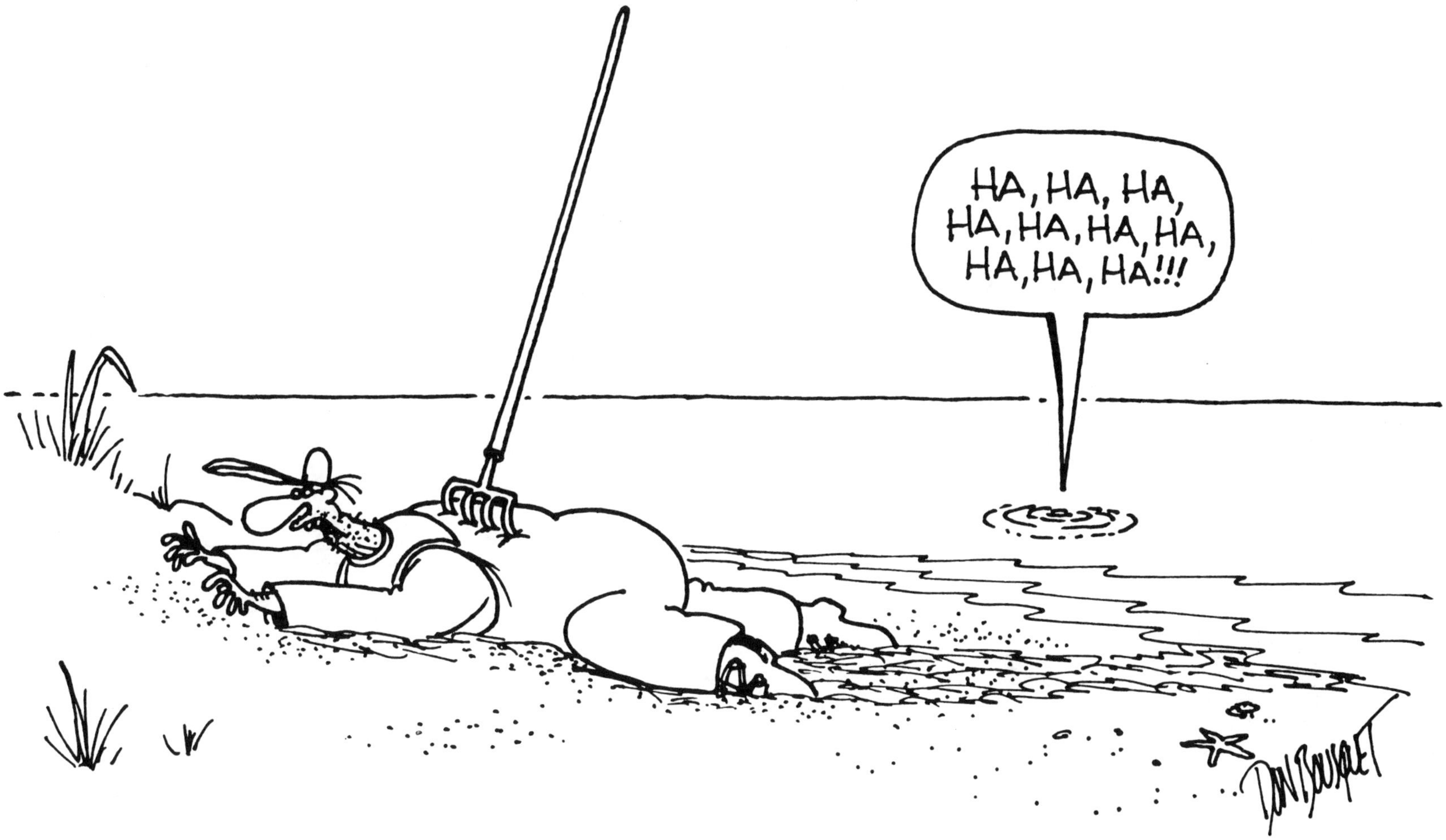
HA, HA, HA,
HA, HA, HA, HA,
HA, HA, HA!!!
DON BOUSQUET

REVENGE OF THE QUAHOG

ONE, TWO, ONE, TWO... C'MON, VINNY! LEMME SEE THAT FOOT MOVE!!!

CLAMAEROBICS

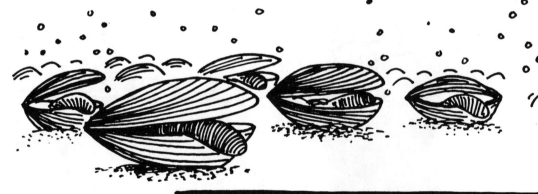

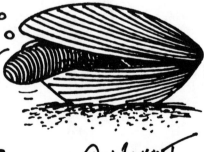

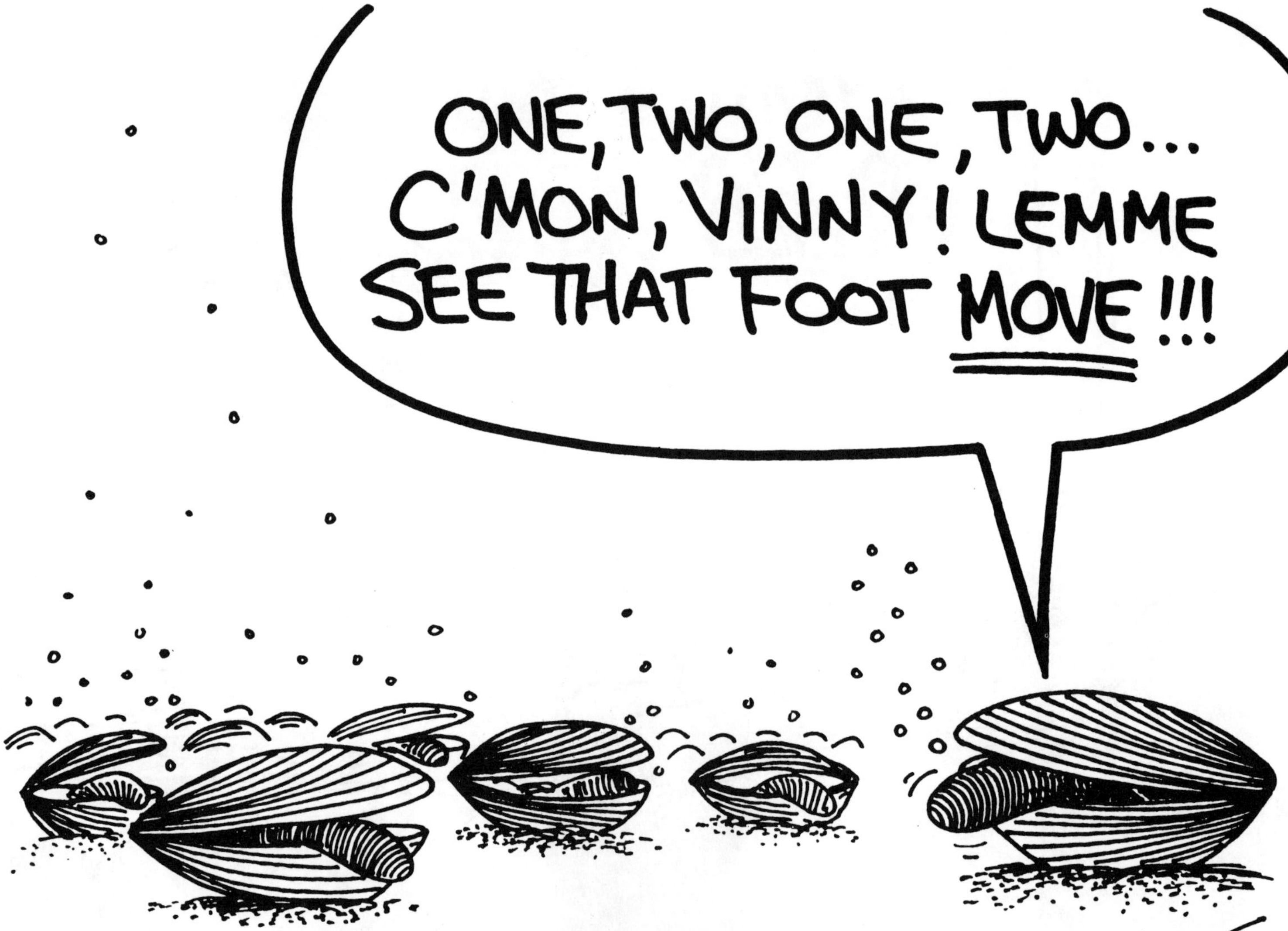

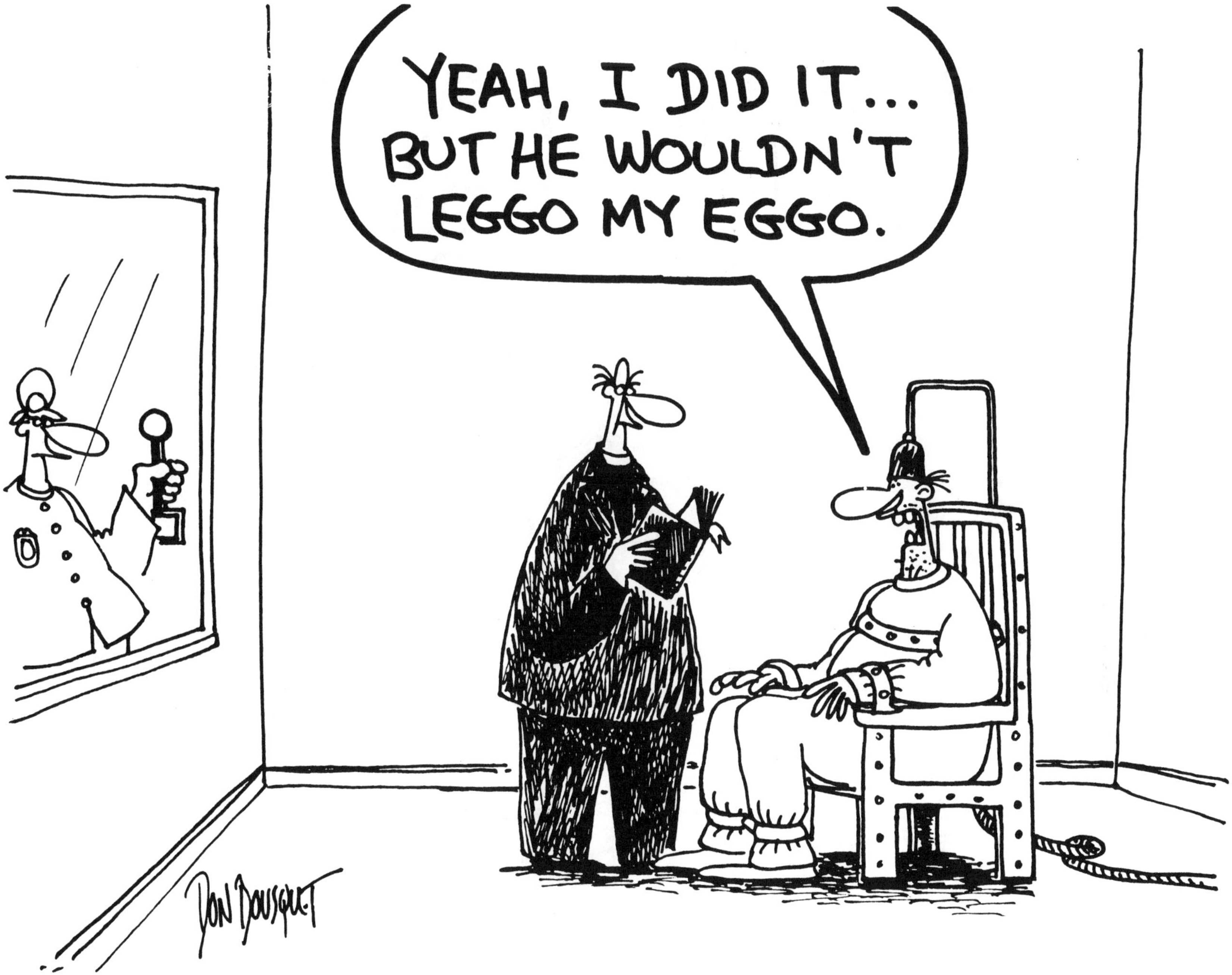
YEAH, I DID IT... BUT HE WOULDN'T LEGGO MY EGGO.
DON BOUSQUET

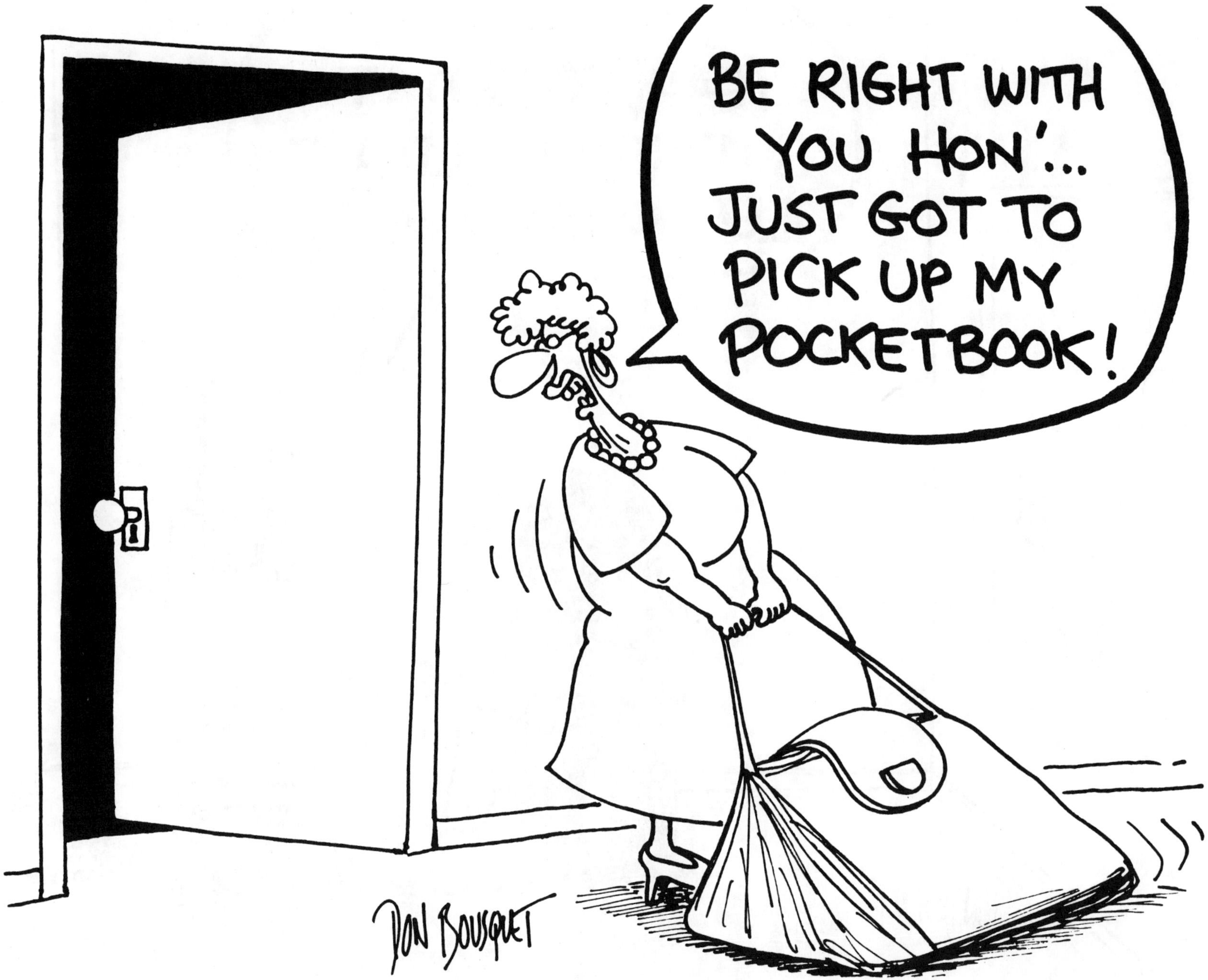
BE RIGHT WITH YOU HON'... JUST GOT TO PICK UP MY POCKETBOOK!
DON BOUSQUET

ACTUALLY, I WAS ALMOST COMPLETELY BALD AND THEN IT HIT ME.... WITH A LITTLE WORK I COULD TRAIN MY EAR HAIR!!!

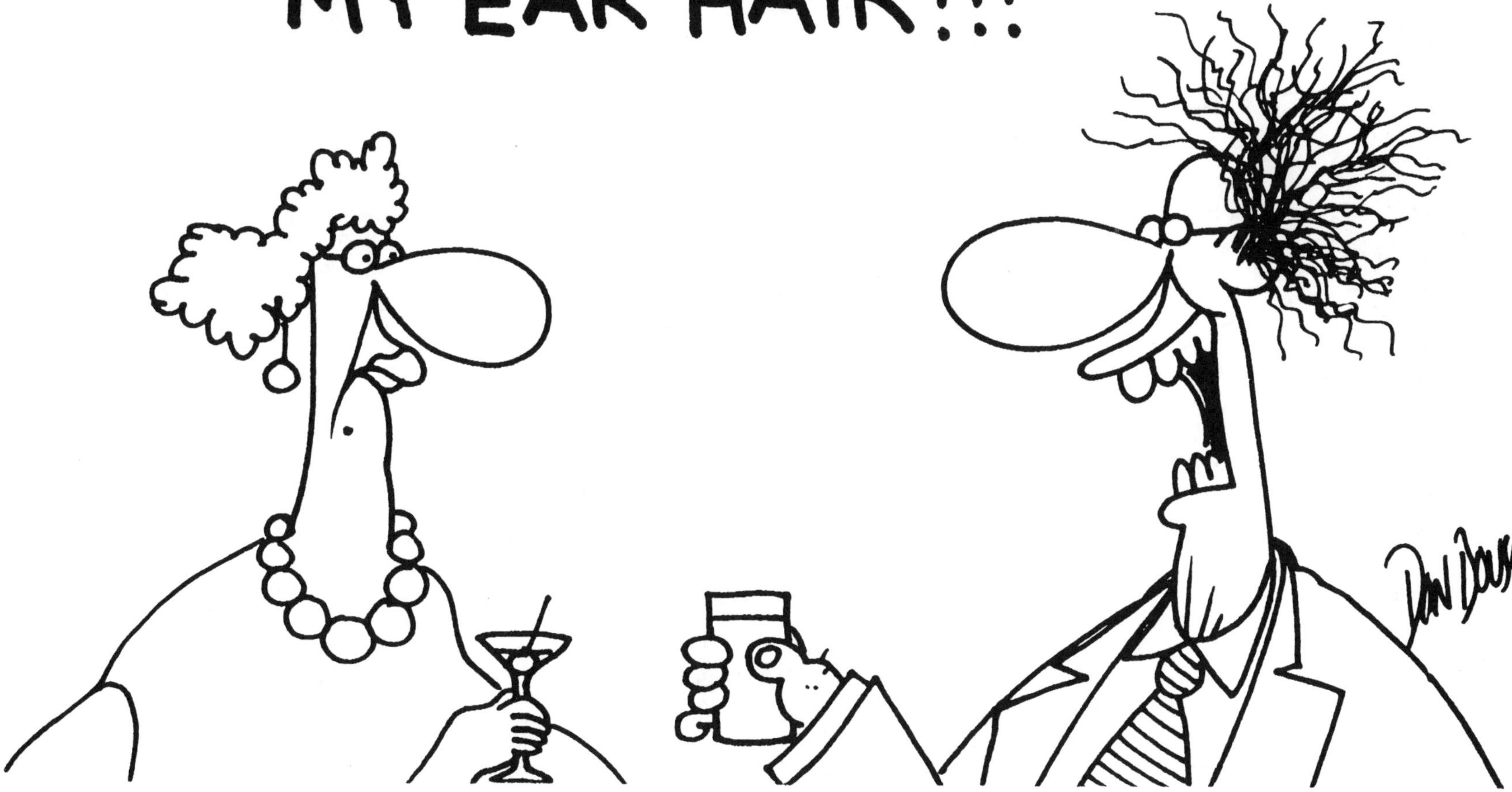

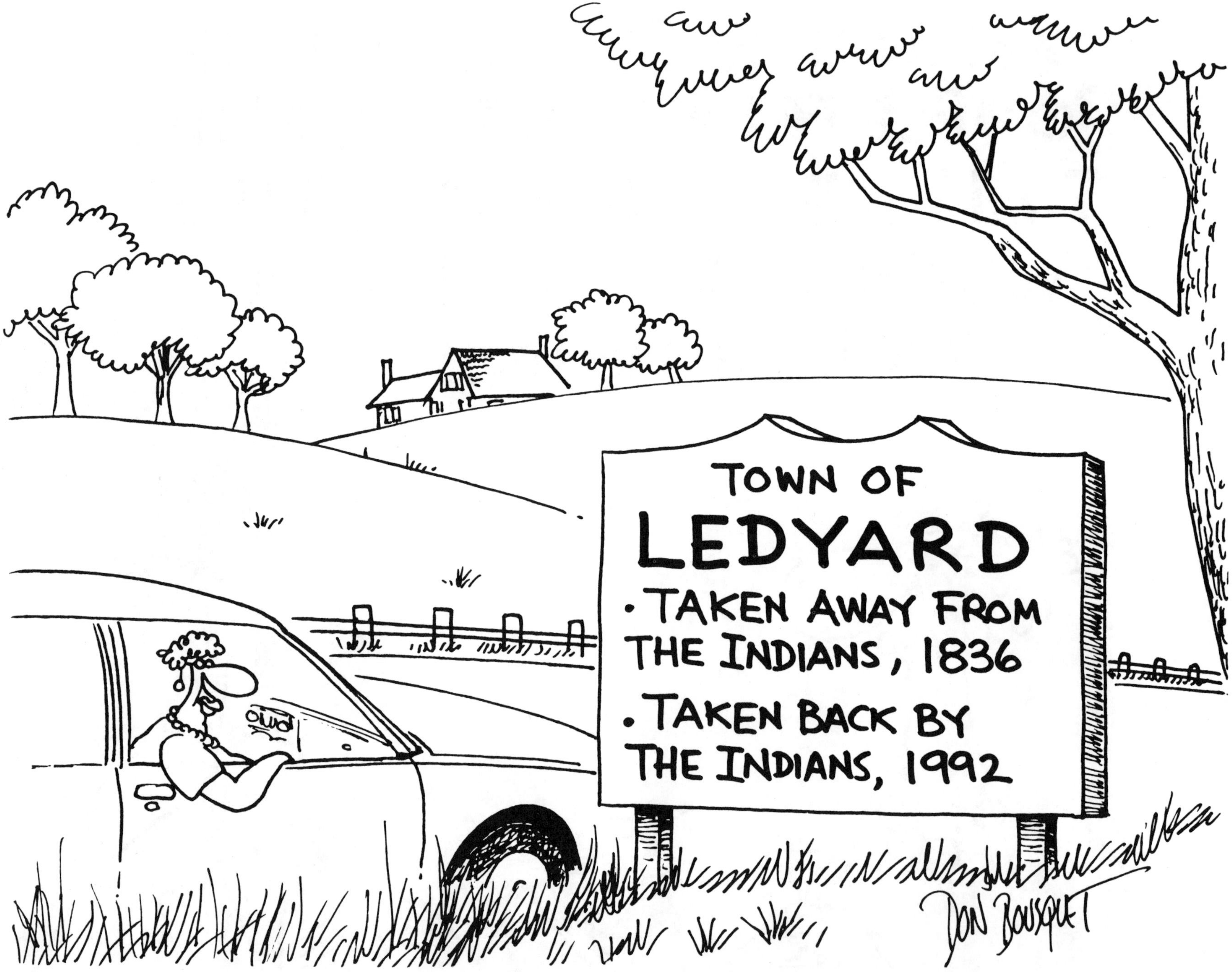
TOWN OF
LEDYARD
• TAKEN AWAY FROM THE INDIANS, 1836
• TAKEN BACK BY THE INDIANS, 1992
DON BOUSQUET

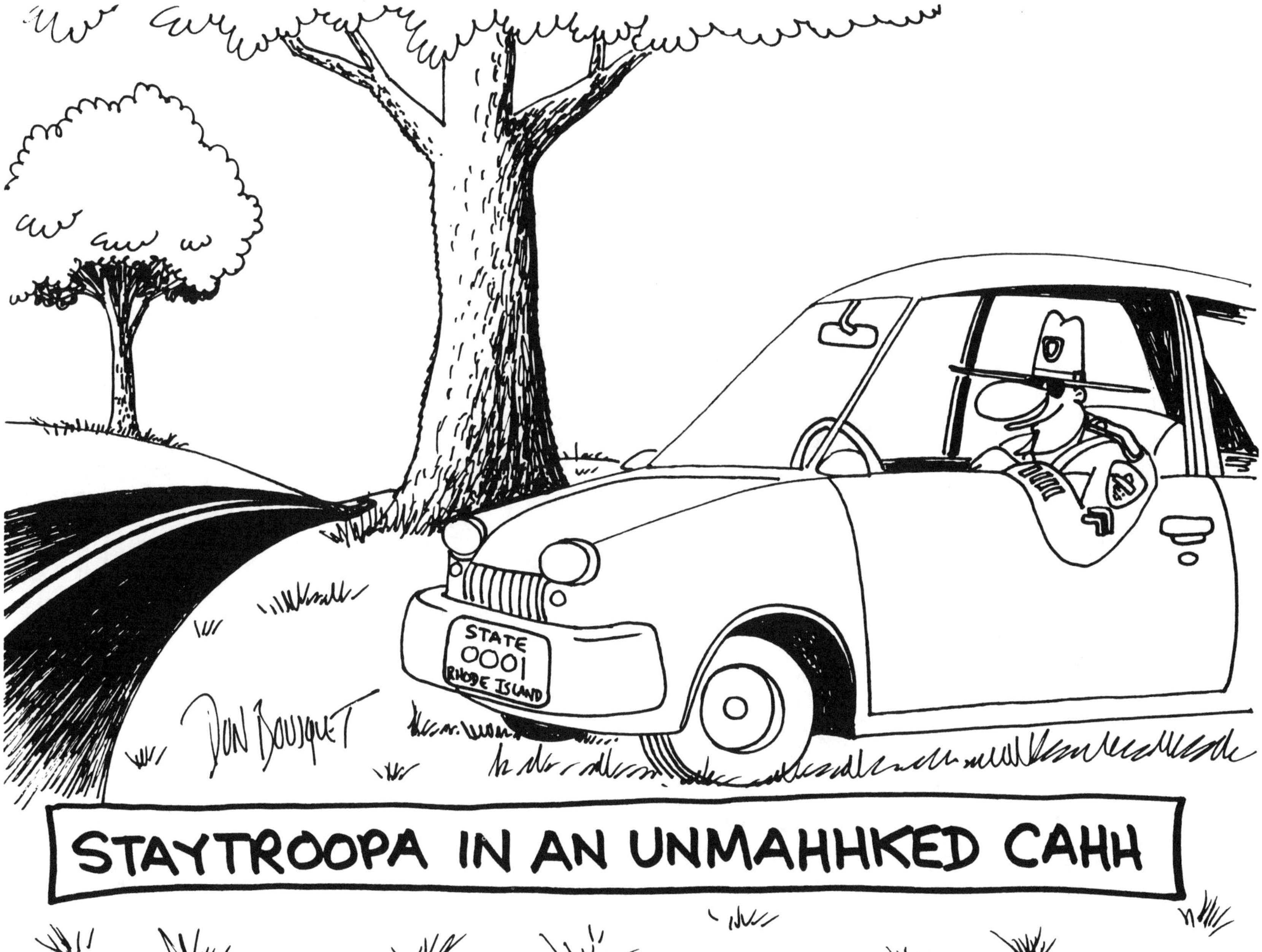
STATE
0001
RHODE ISLAND
DON BOUSQUET

STAYTROOPA IN AN UNMAHHKED CAHH

WHEN POPULAR PROVIDENCE BUSINESSES MERGE...

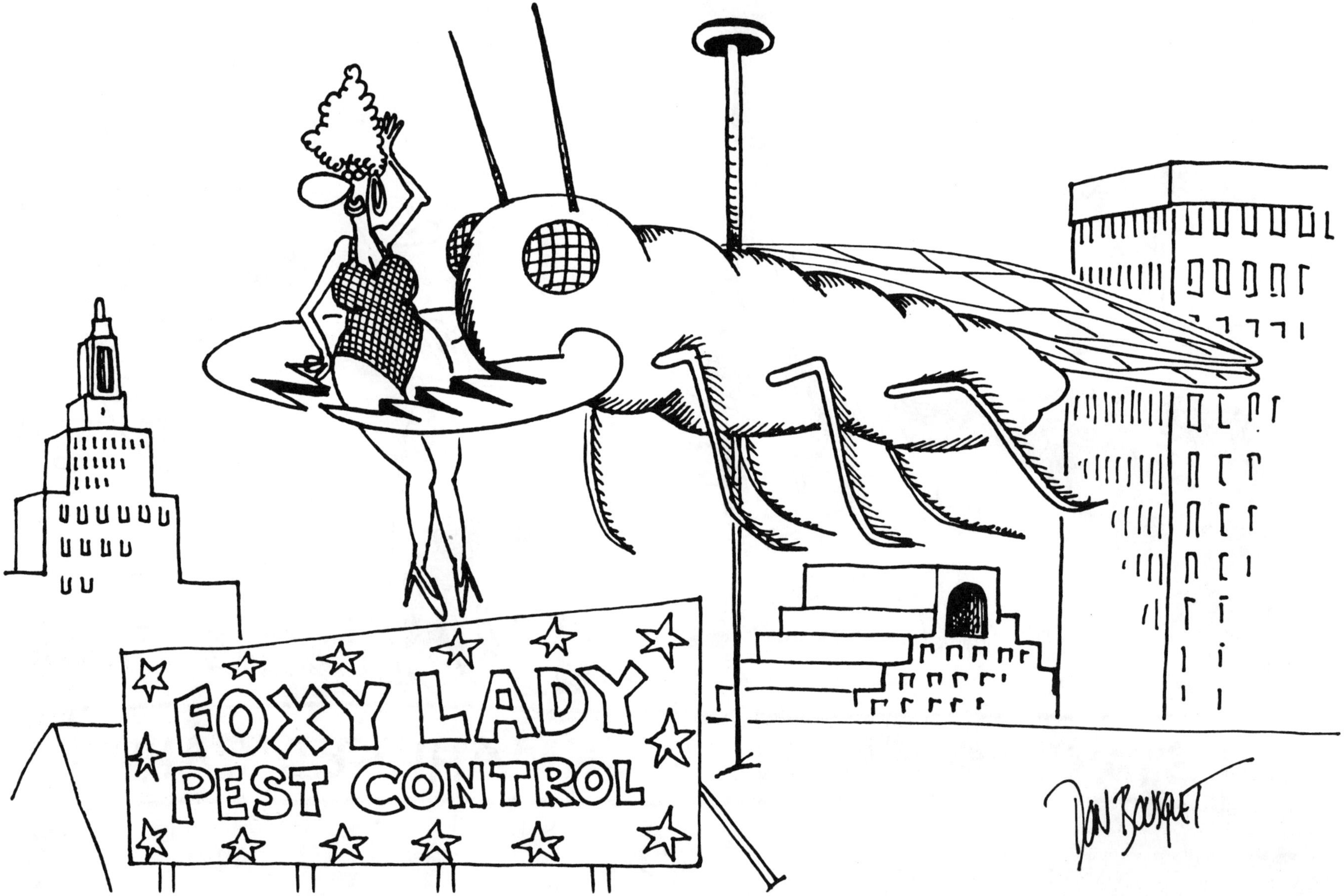
FOXY LADY
PEST CONTROL
DON BOUSQUET

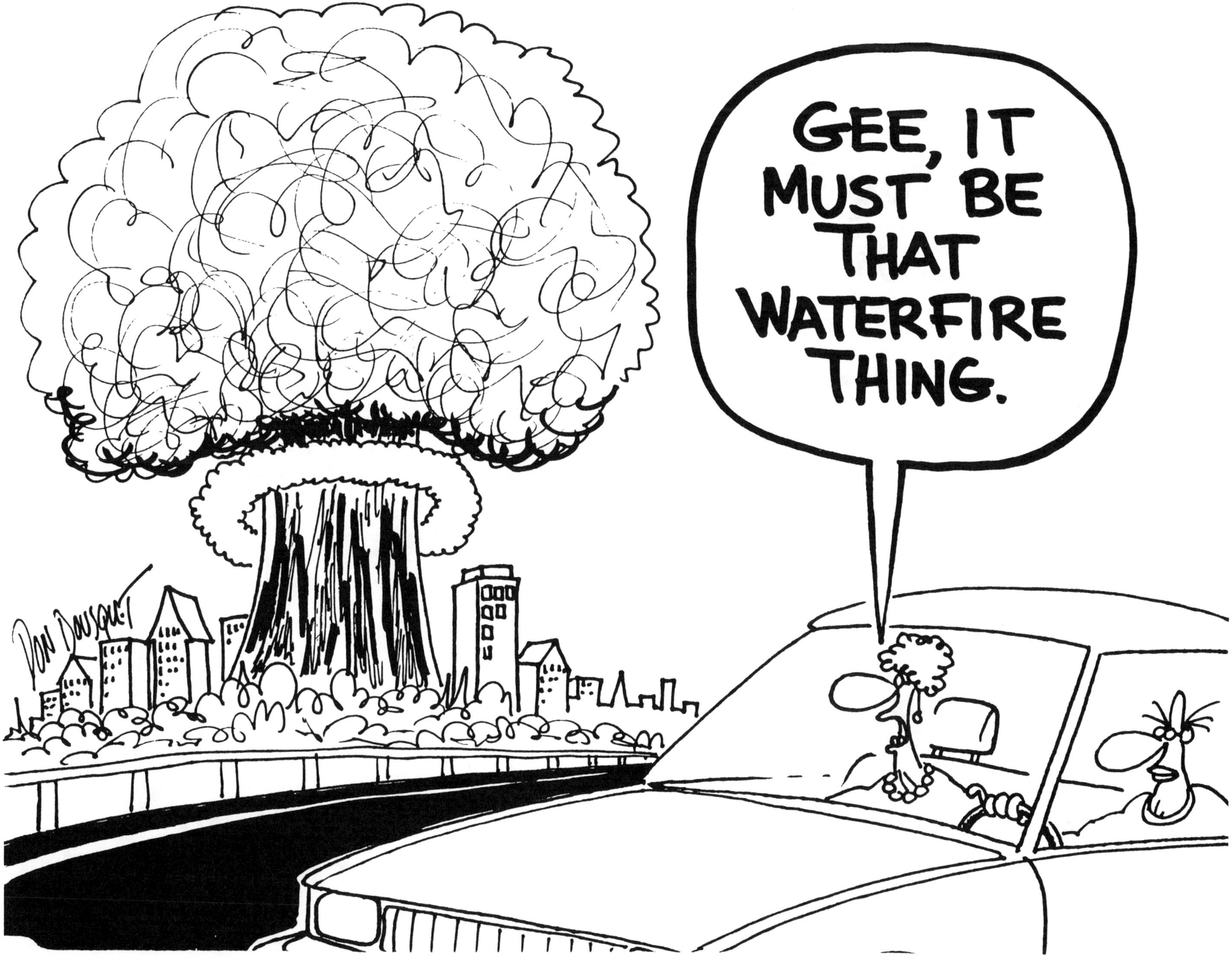
GEE, IT MUST BE THAT WATERFIRE THING.

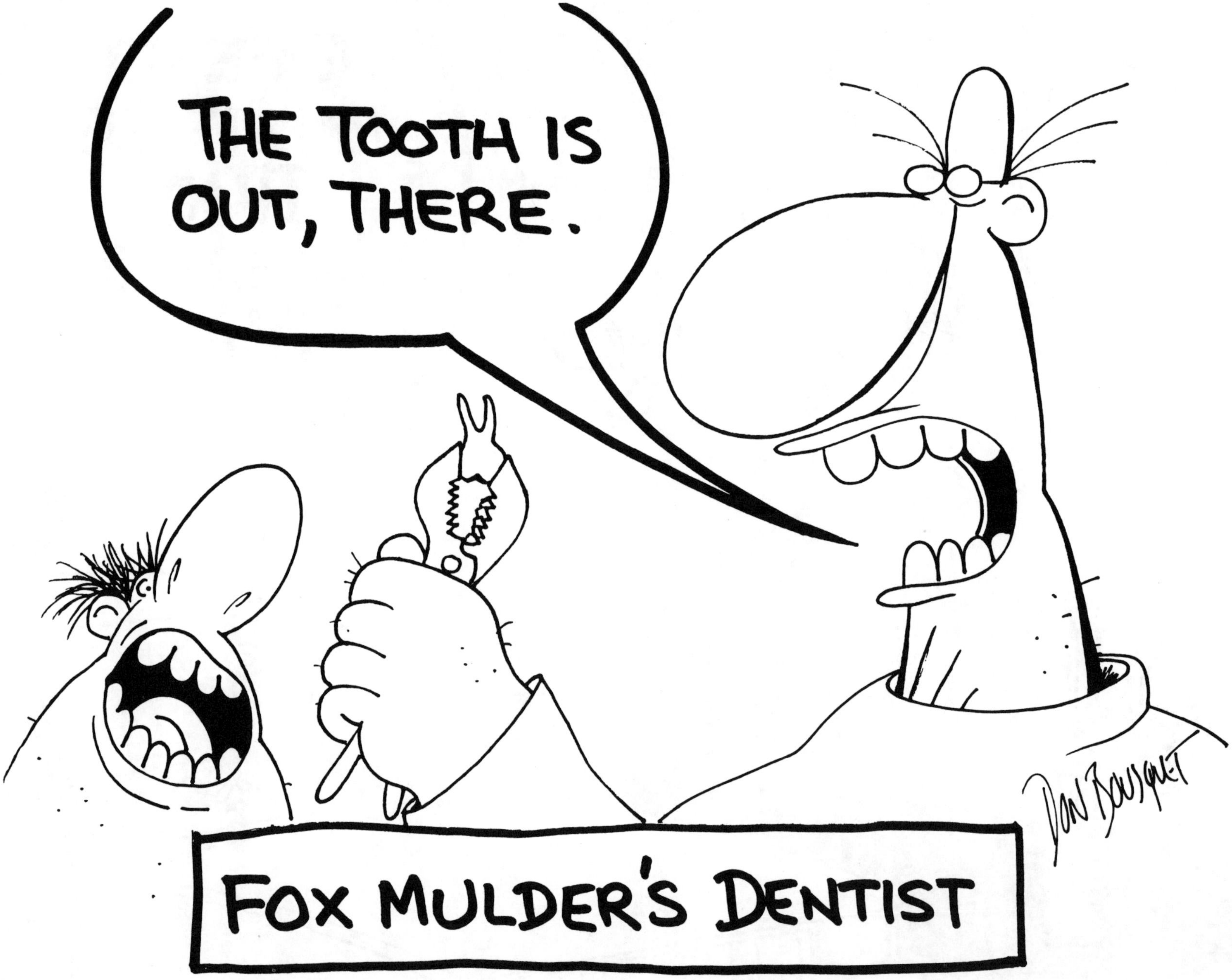
THE TOOTH IS OUT, THERE.
DON BOUSQUET
FOX MULDER'S DENTIST

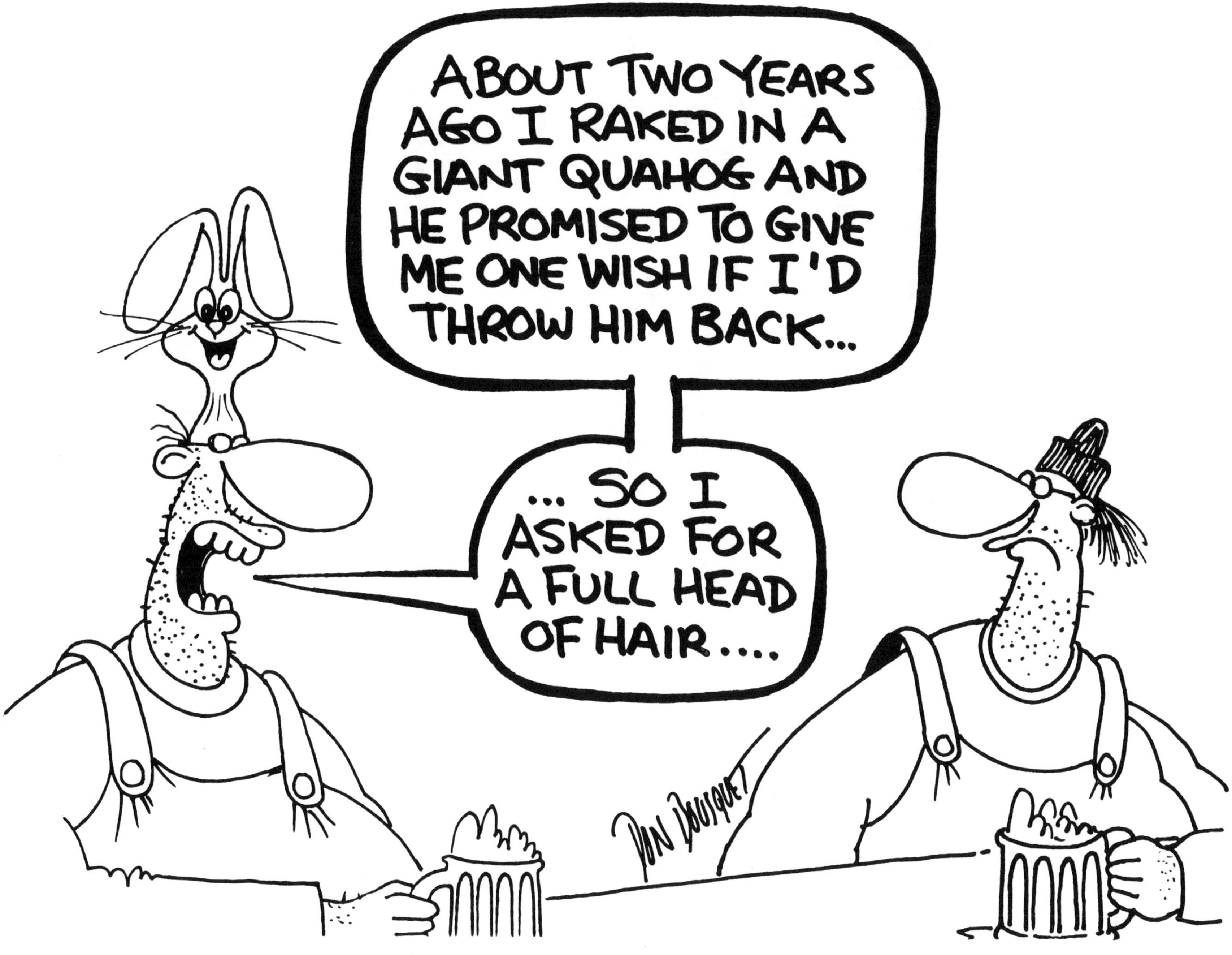
ABOUT TWO YEARS AGO I RAKED IN A GIANT QUAHOG AND HE PROMISED TO GIVE ME ONE WISH IF I'D THROW HIM BACK...
... SO I ASKED FOR A FULL HEAD OF HAIR....

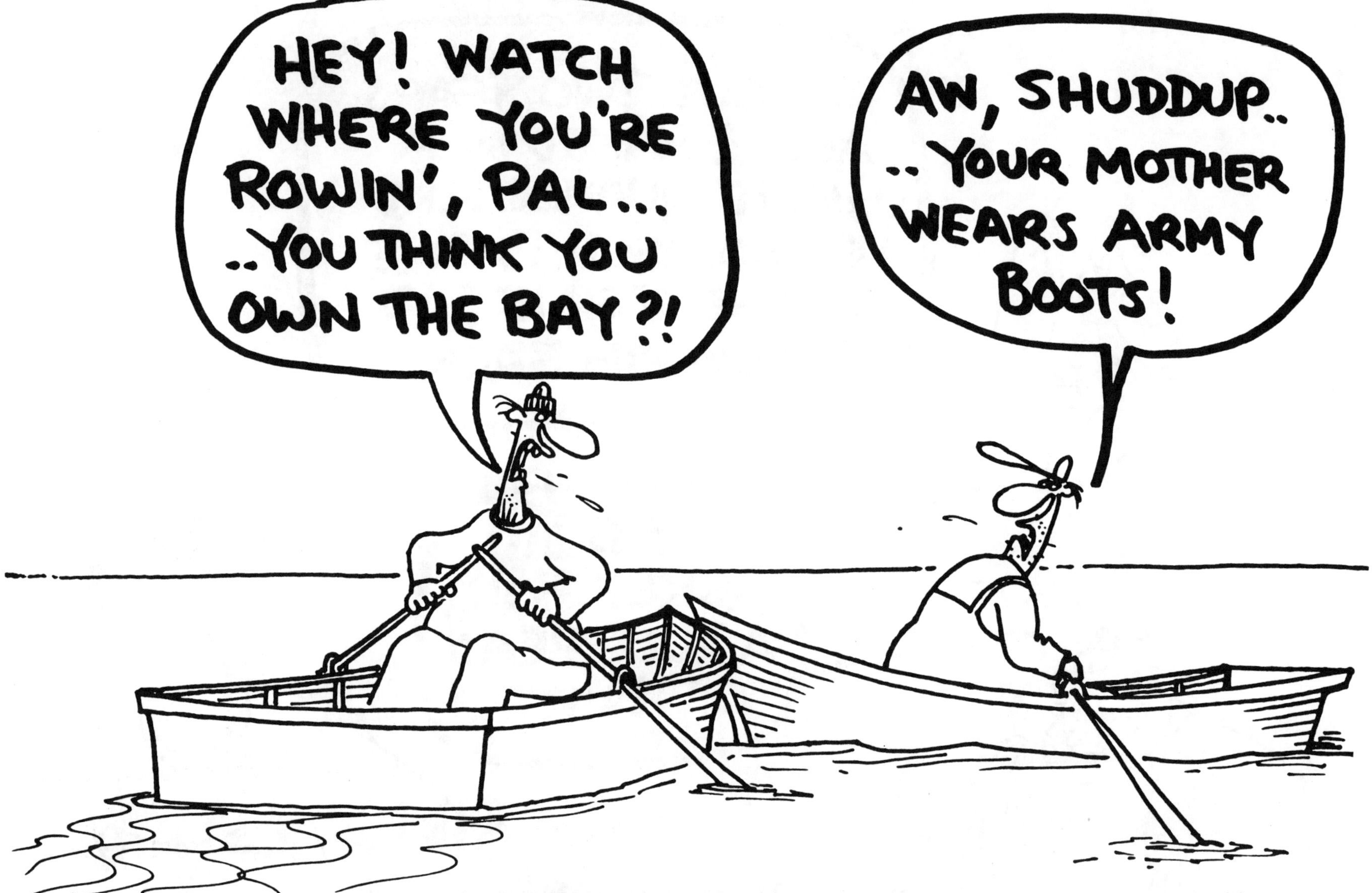
HEY! WATCH WHERE YOU'RE ROWIN', PAL... ..YOU THINK YOU OWN THE BAY?!
AW, SHUDDUP.. ..YOUR MOTHER WEARS ARMY BOOTS!
DON BOUSQUET

ROW RAGE

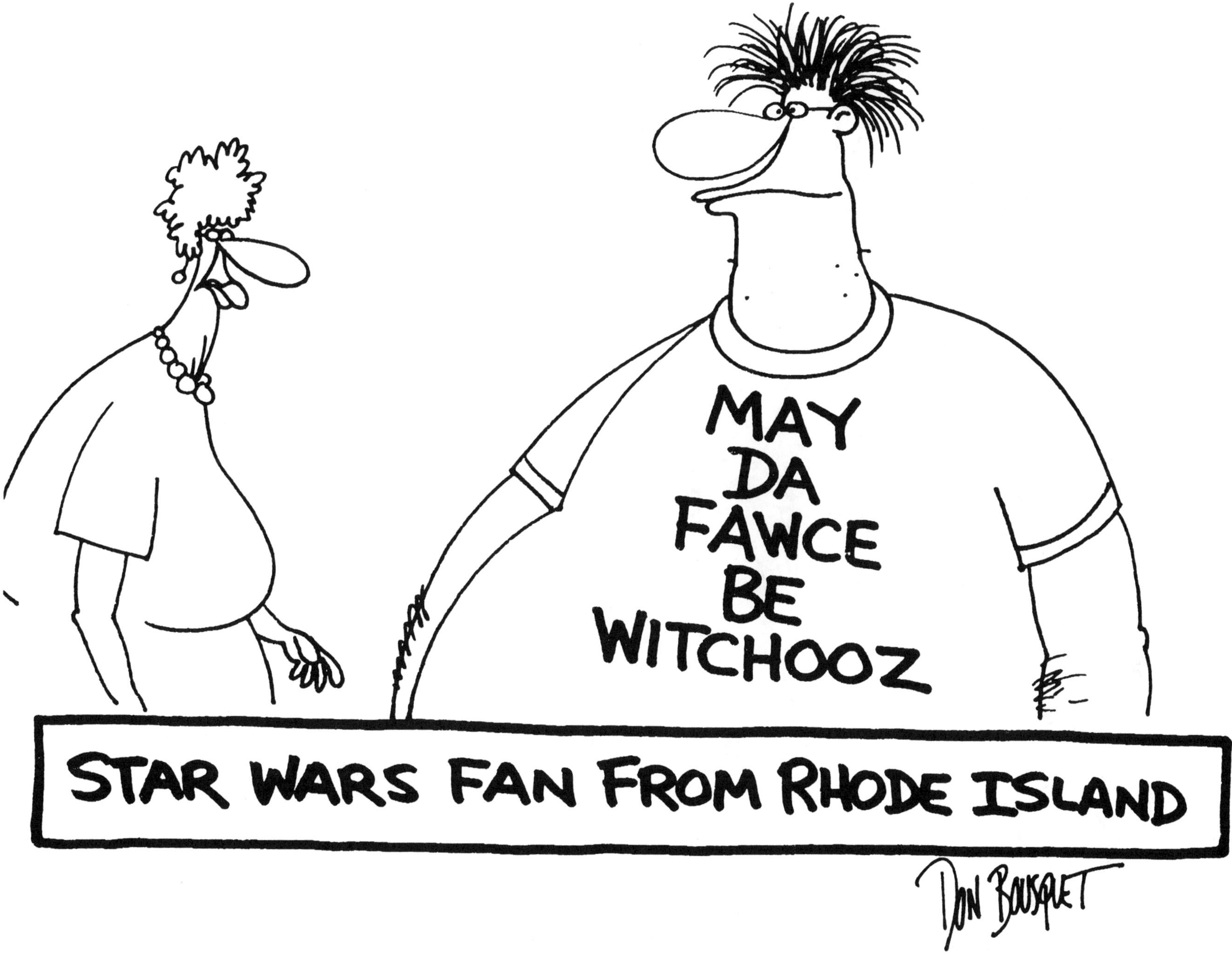
MAY DA FAWCE BE WITCHOOZ
DON BOUSQUET

STAR WARS FAN FROM RHODE ISLAND

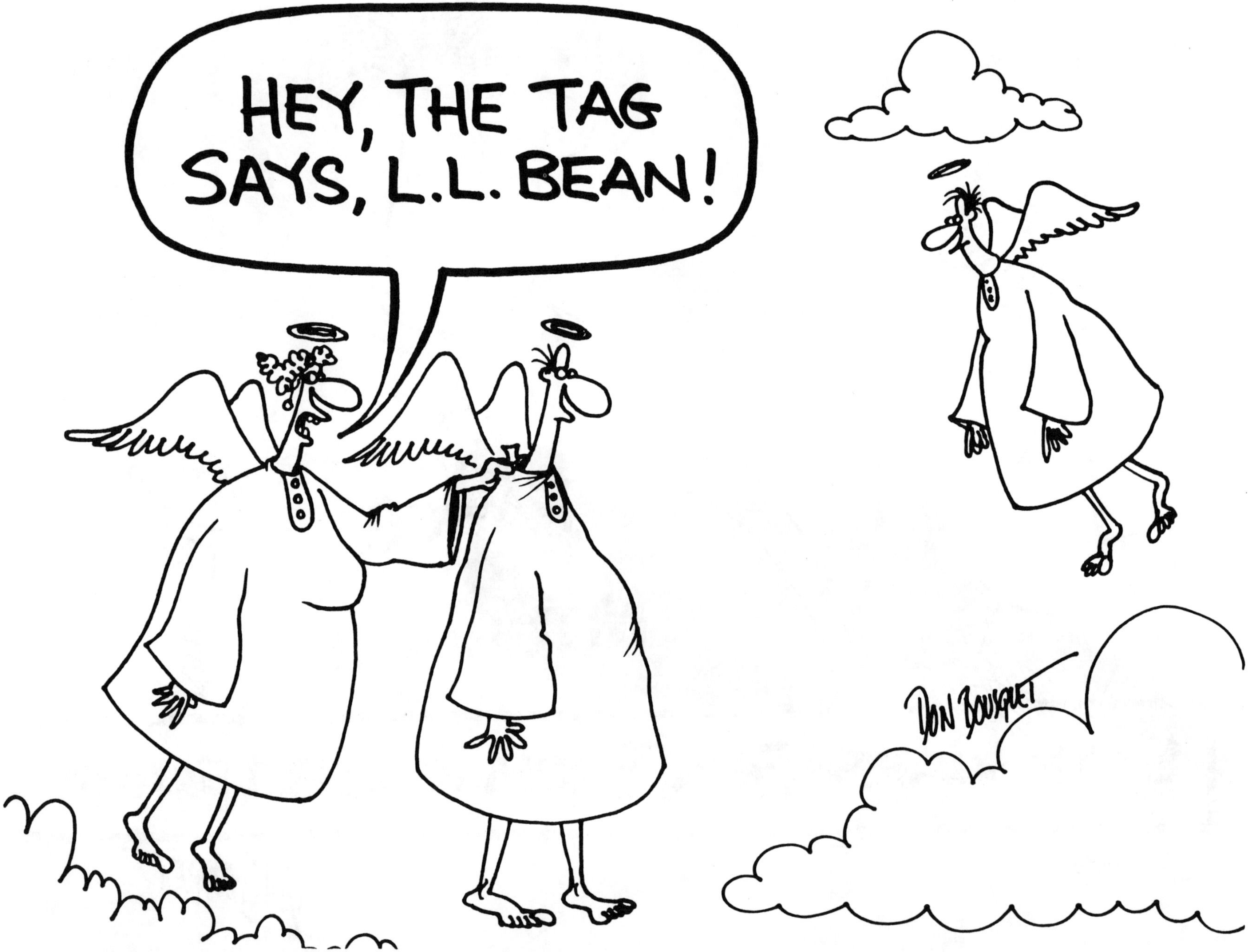
HEY, THE TAG SAYS, L.L. BEAN!
DON BOUSQUET

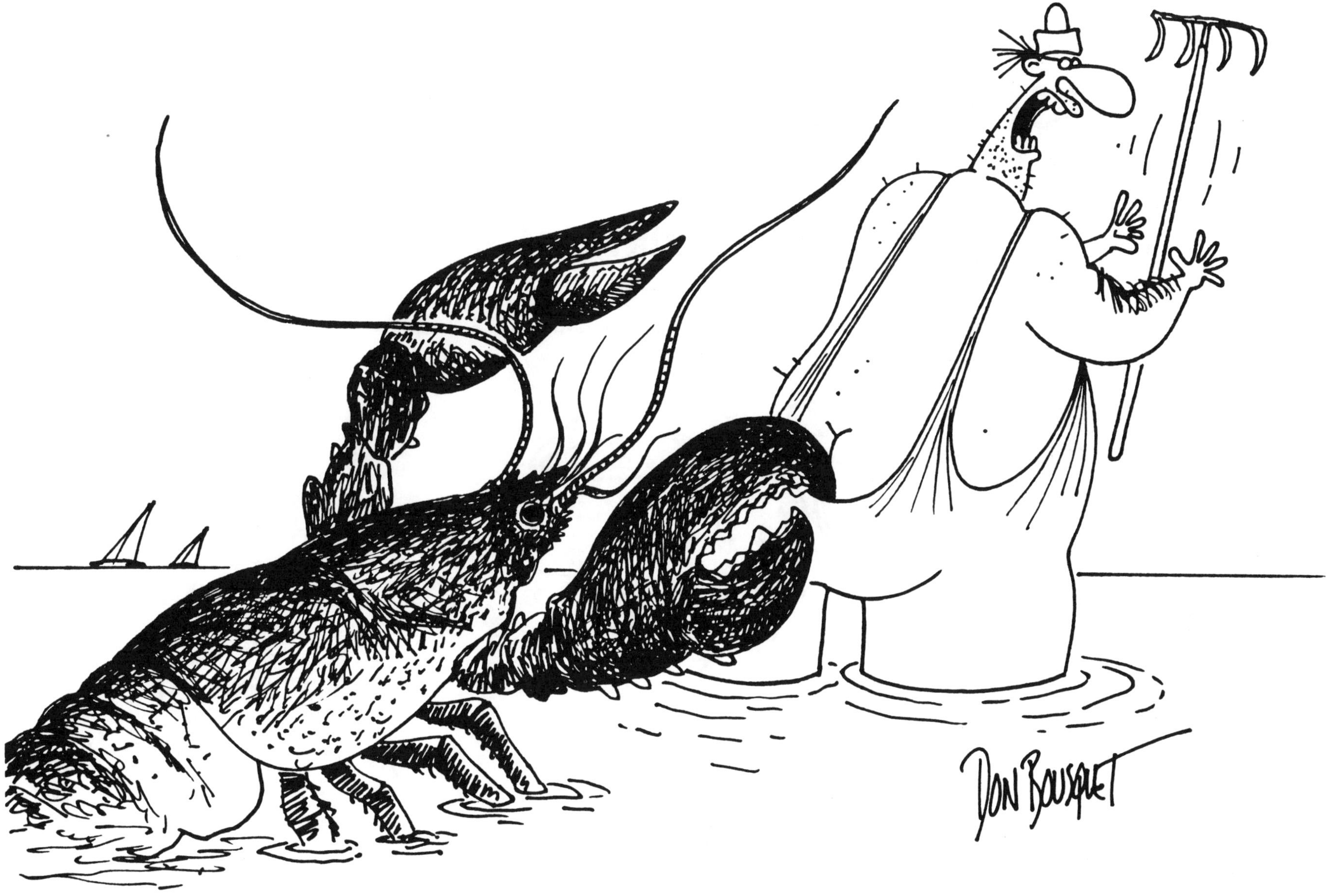
DON BOUSQUET

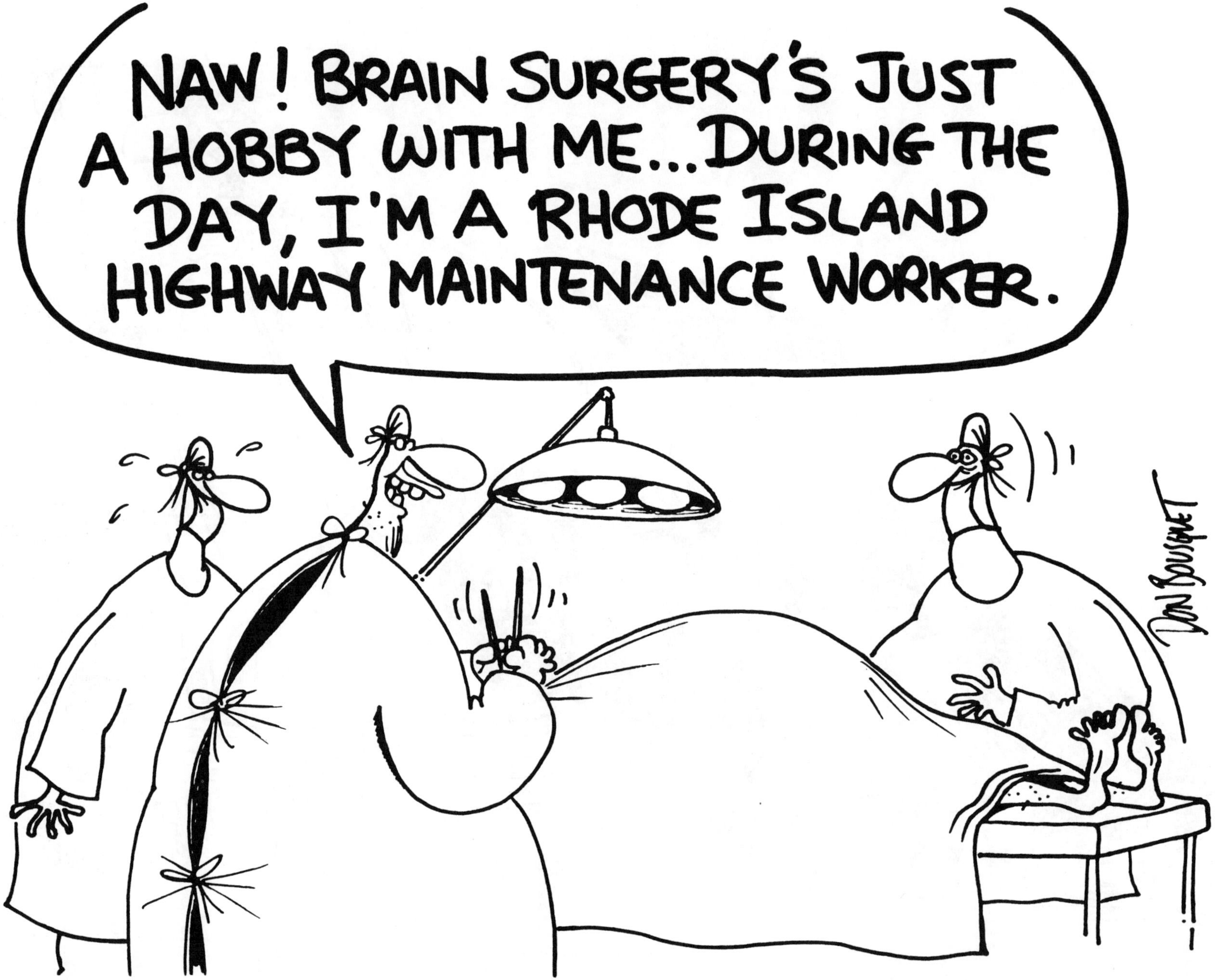
NAW! BRAIN SURGERY'S JUST A HOBBY WITH ME...DURING THE DAY, I'M A RHODE ISLAND HIGHWAY MAINTENANCE WORKER.
DAN BOUSQUET

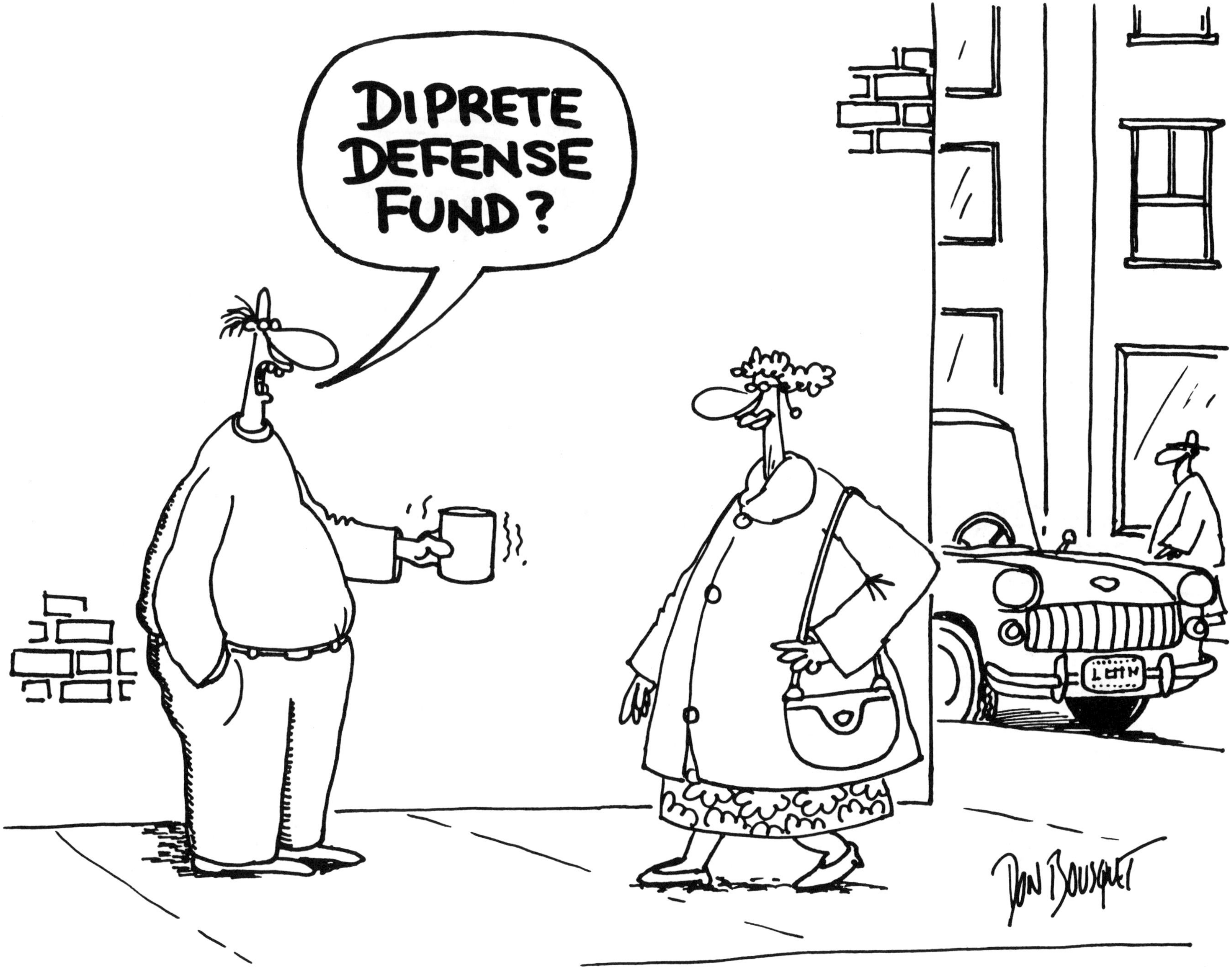
DI PRETE DEFENSE FUND?
DON BOUSQUET

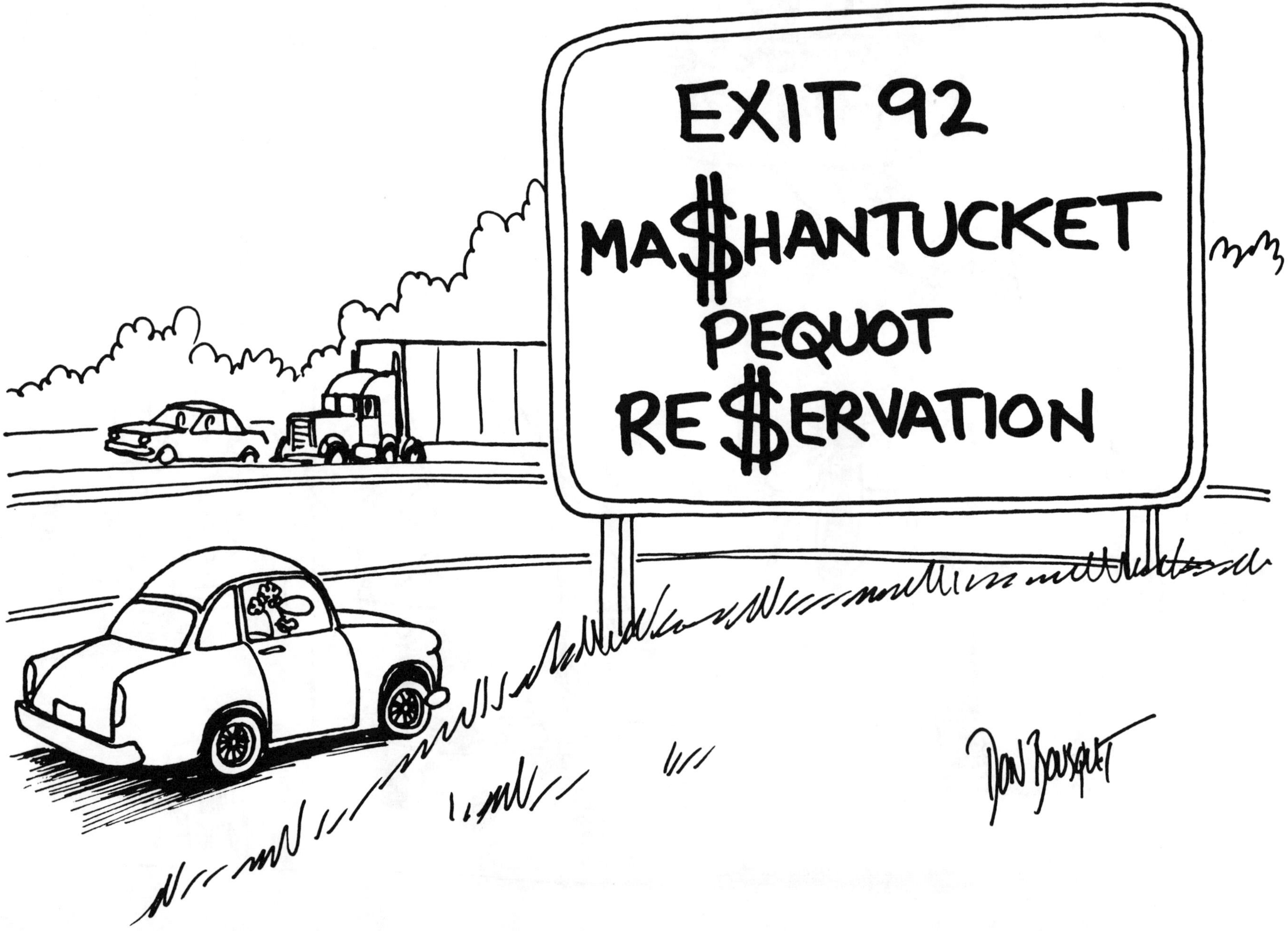
EXIT 92
MA$HANTUCKET
PEQUOT
RE$ERVATION
DON BOUSQUET

SEQUEL TO THE FILM CLASSIC, "THE FLY."..."THE FLY MEETS THE LADYBUG"

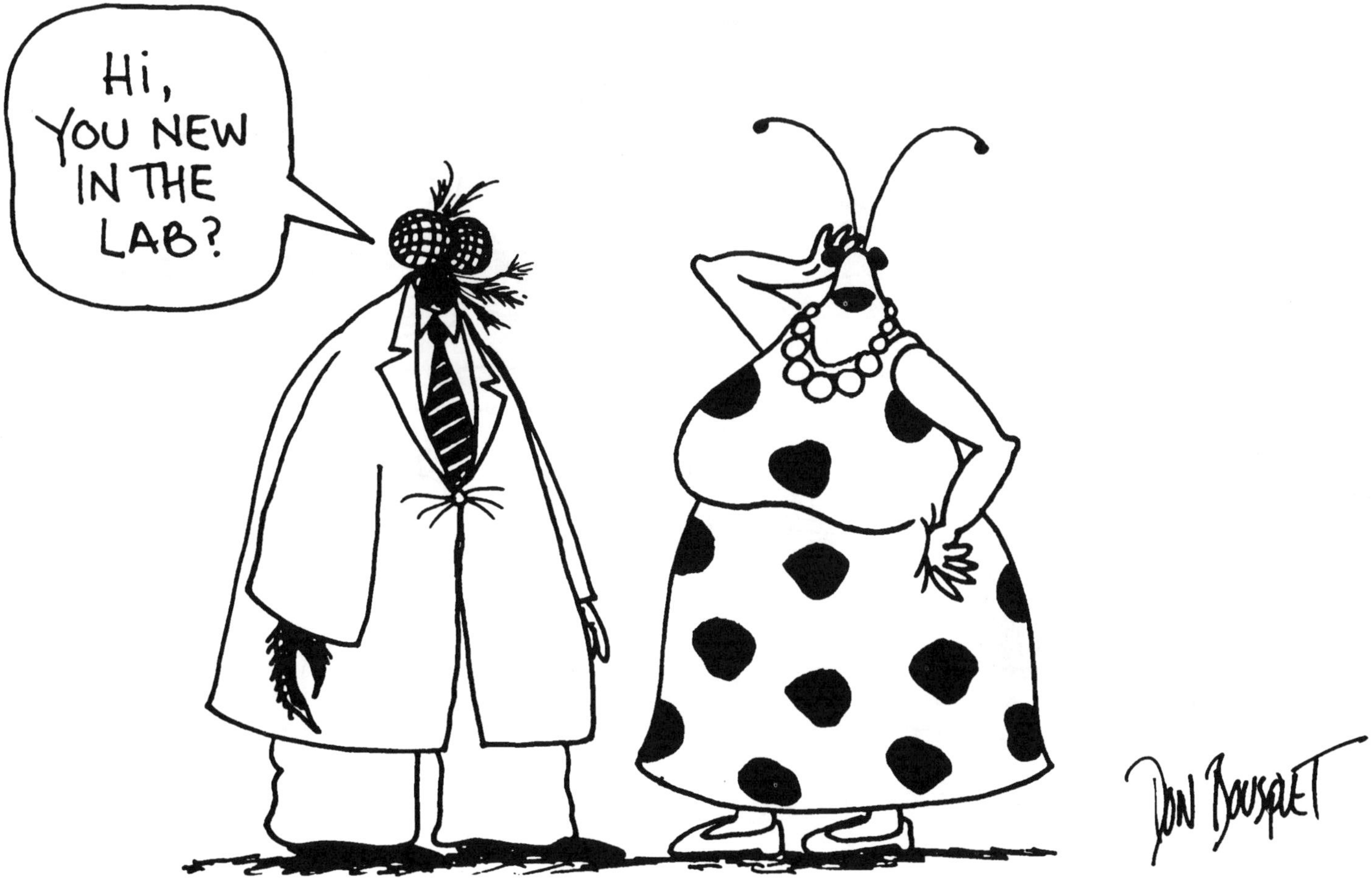
Hi, YOU NEW IN THE LAB?
DON BOUSQUET

RHODE ISLAND EXITS

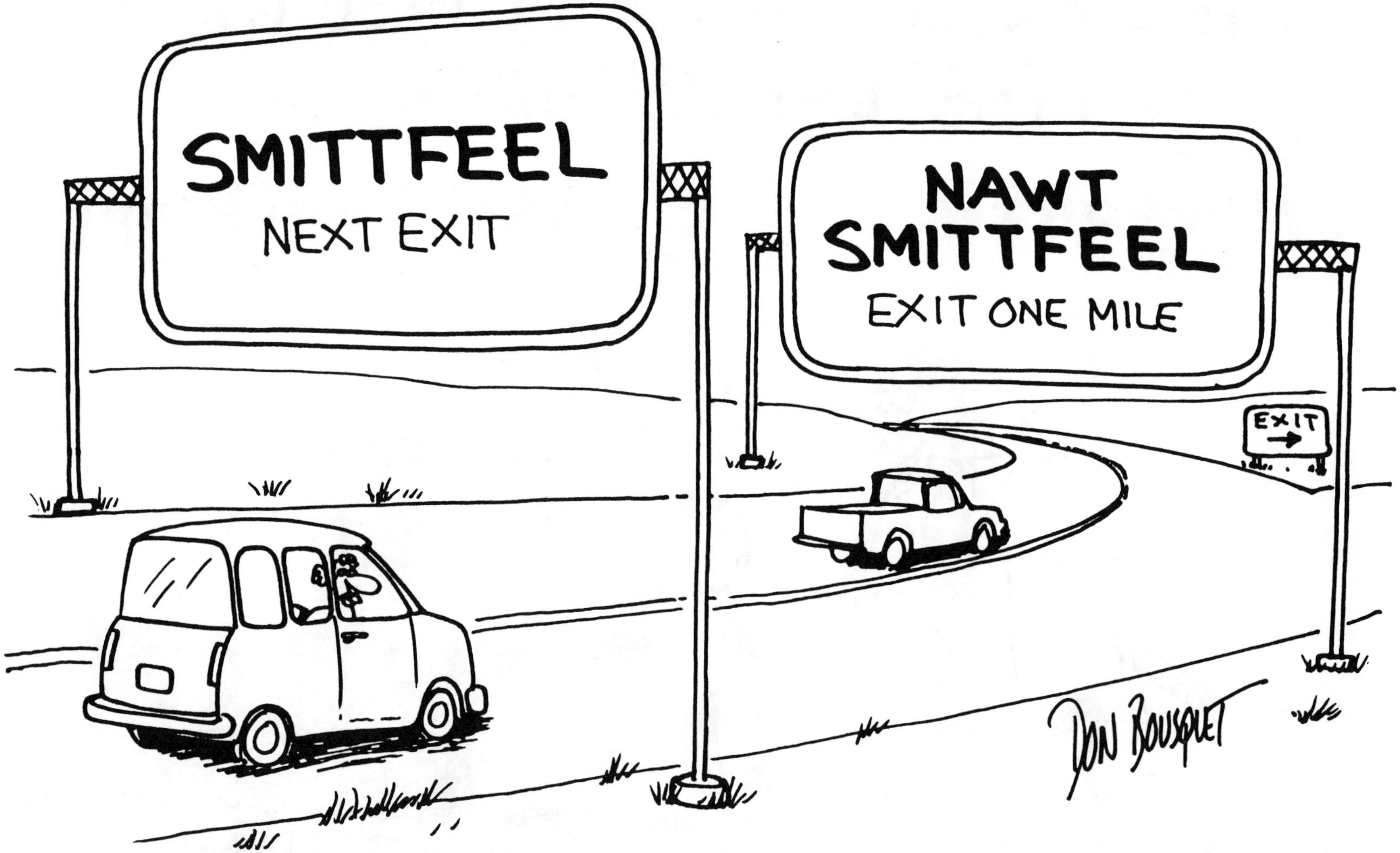
SMITTFEEL
NEXT EXIT
NAWT SMITTFEEL
EXIT ONE MILE
EXIT
DON BOUSQUET

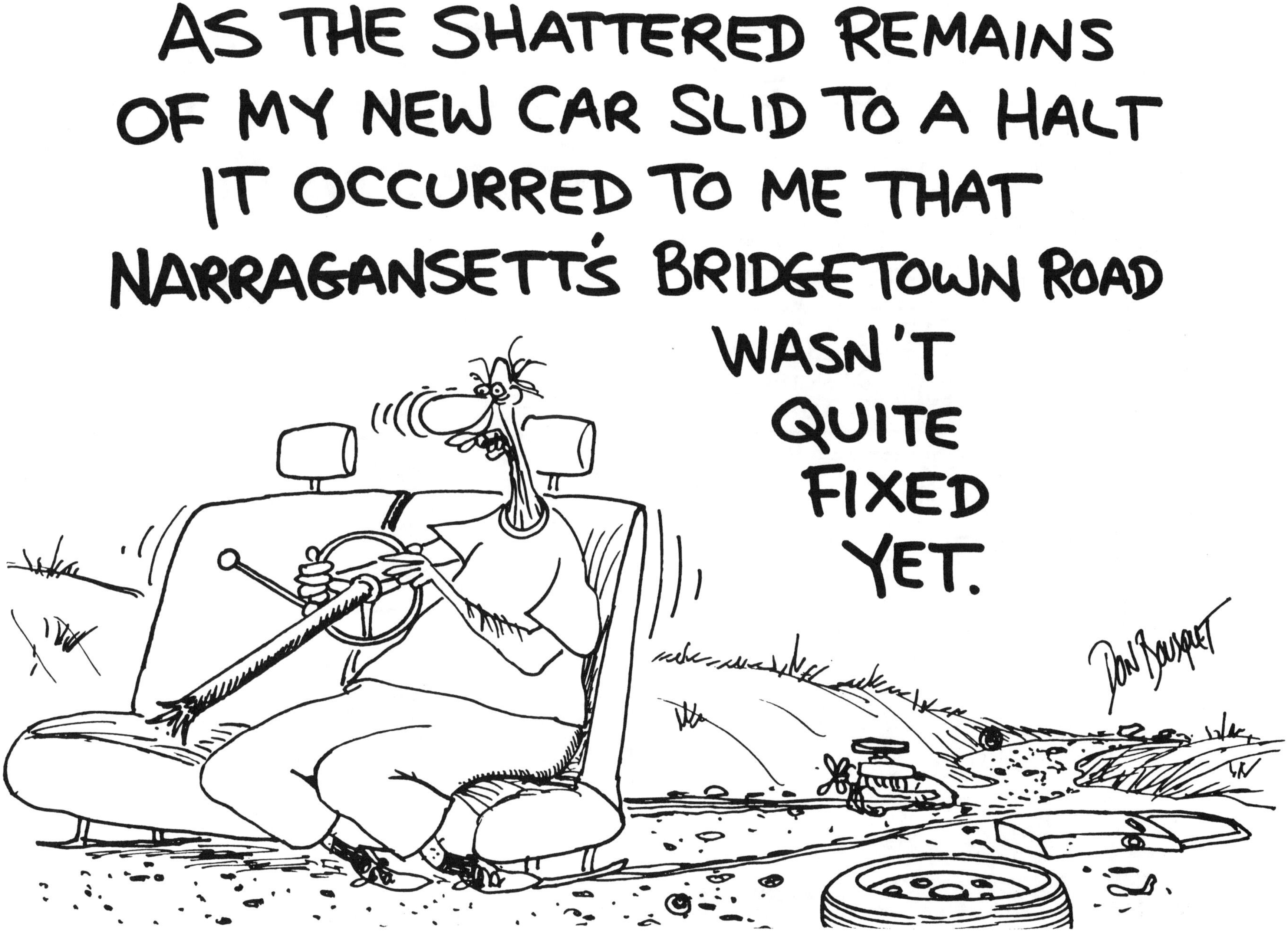
AS THE SHATTERED REMAINS OF MY NEW CAR SLID TO A HALT IT OCCURRED TO ME THAT NARRAGANSETT'S BRIDGETOWN ROAD WASN'T QUITE FIXED YET.
DON BOUSQUET

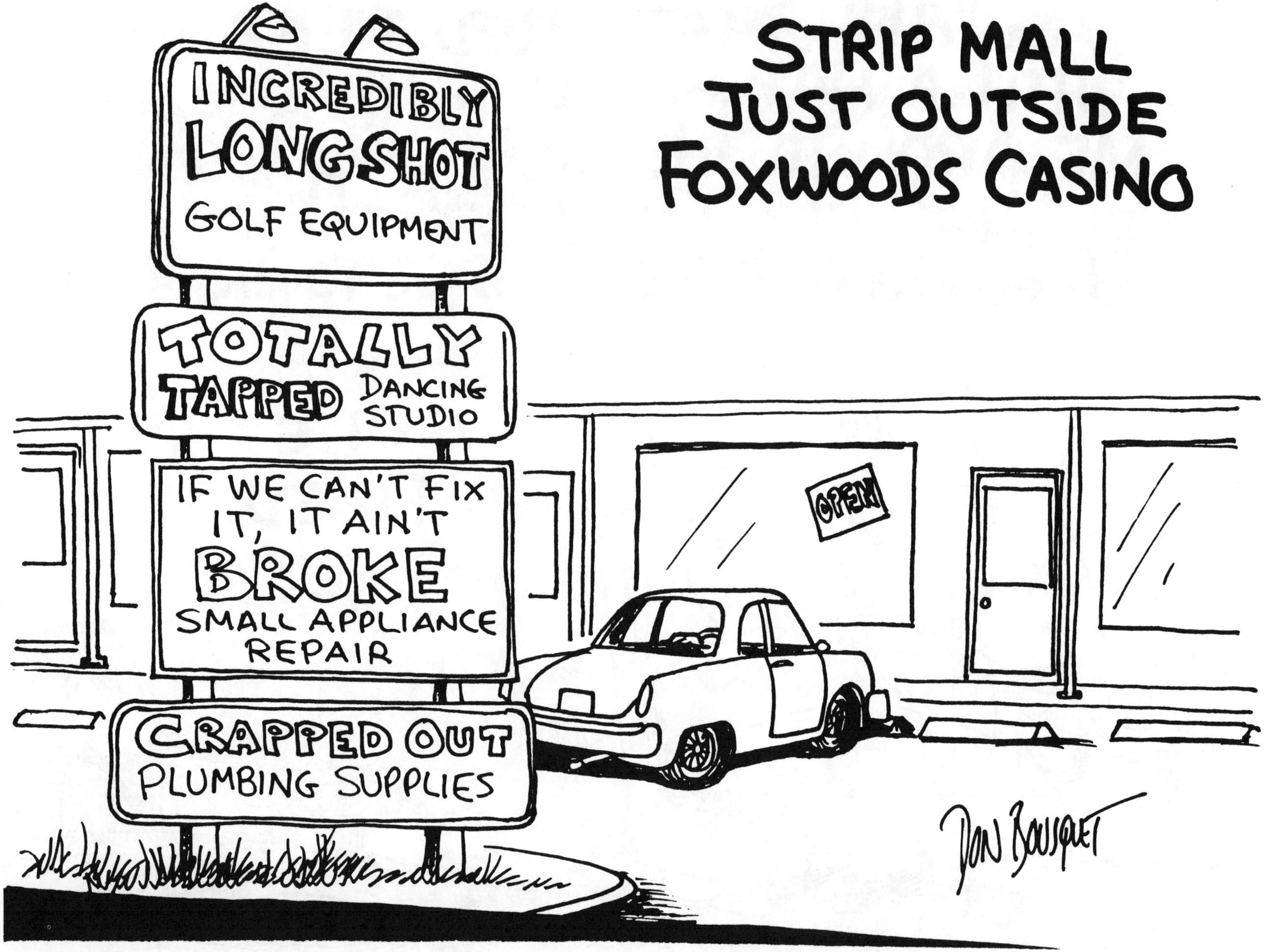
STRIP MALL
JUST OUTSIDE
FOXWOODS CASINO
INCREDIBLY
LONGSHOT
GOLF EQUIPMENT
TOTALLY
TAPPED DANCING STUDIO
IF WE CAN'T FIX IT, IT AIN'T
BROKE
SMALL APPLIANCE REPAIR
CRAPPED OUT
PLUMBING SUPPLIES
OPEN
DON BOUSQUET

... AND THEN THIS GUY WITH A HATCHET IS CHASING ME AROUND THE BARN YARD AND YELLING, 'IT'S NOVEMBER TWENTY-SEVENTH!' I TELL YOU, VINNY, IT WAS THE WEIRDEST DREAM.

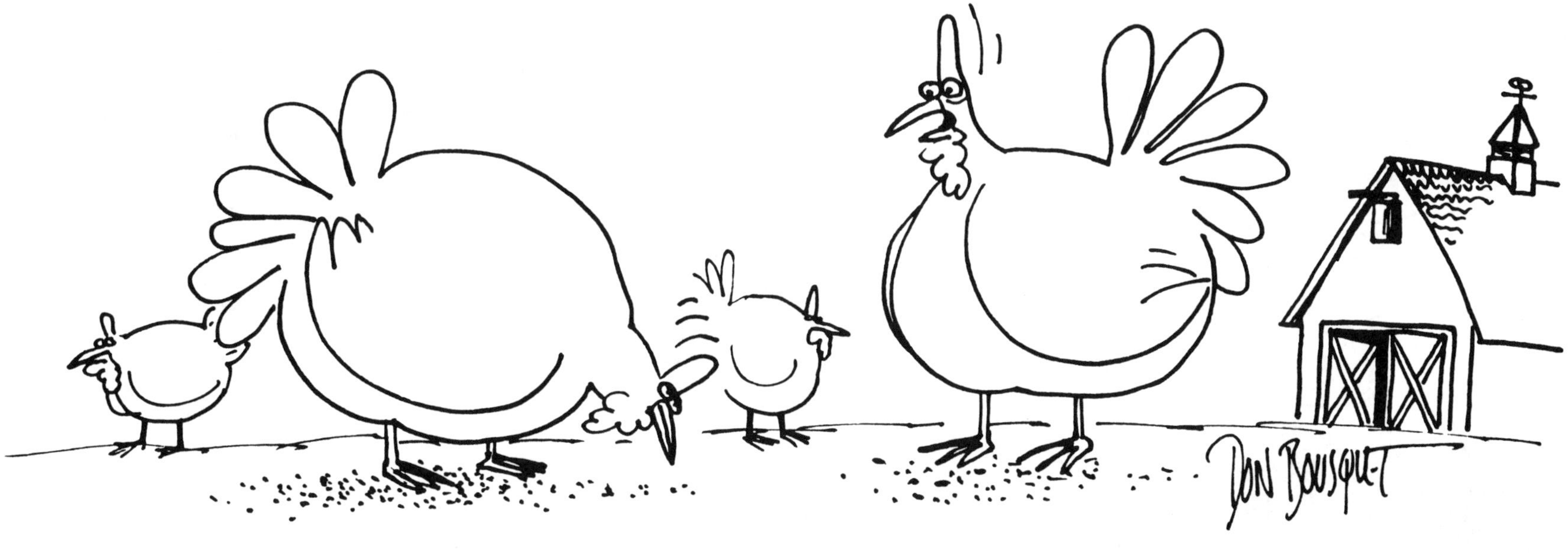
DON BOUSQUET

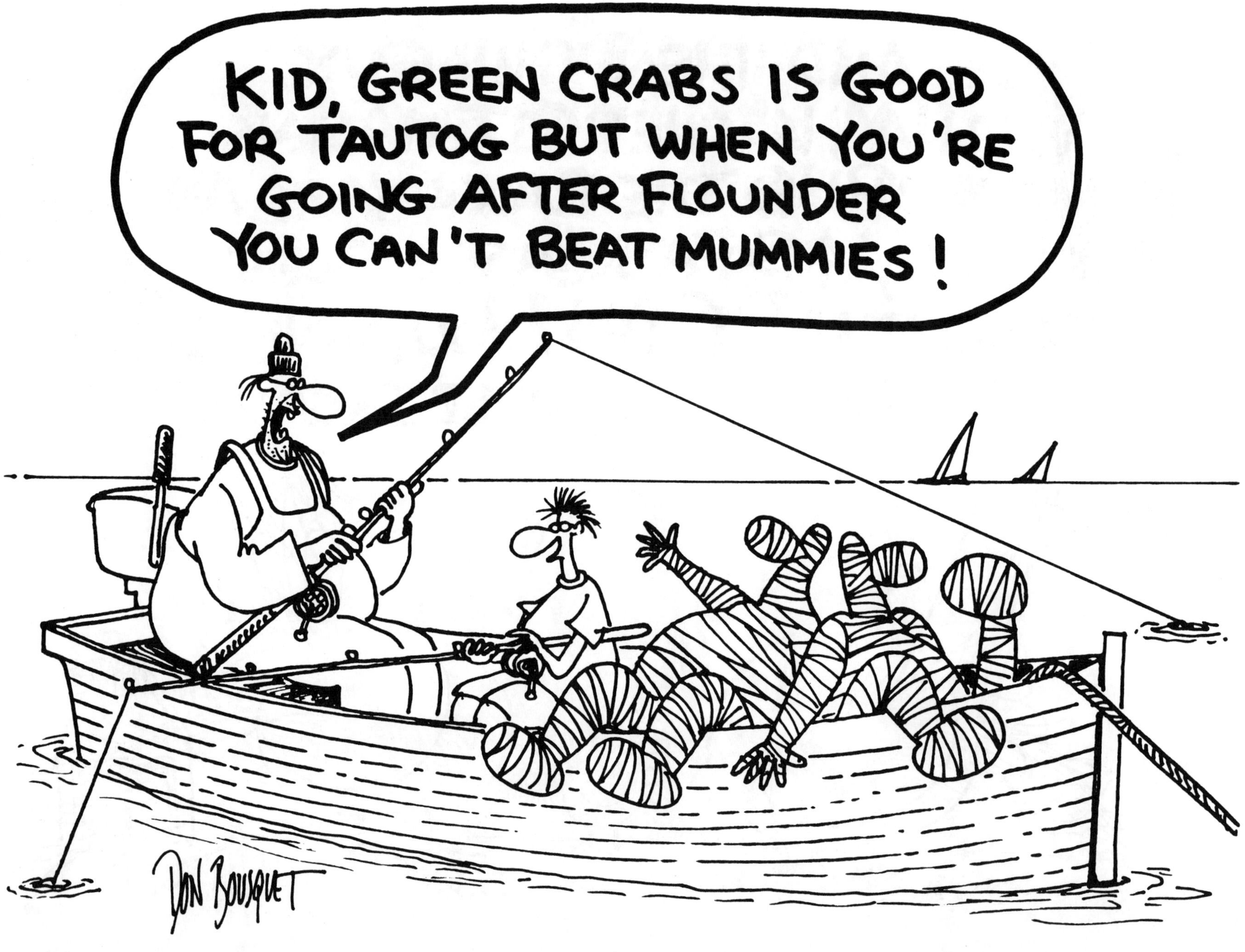
KID, GREEN CRABS IS GOOD FOR TAUTOG BUT WHEN YOU'RE GOING AFTER FLOUNDER YOU CAN'T BEAT MUMMIES!
DON BOUSQUET

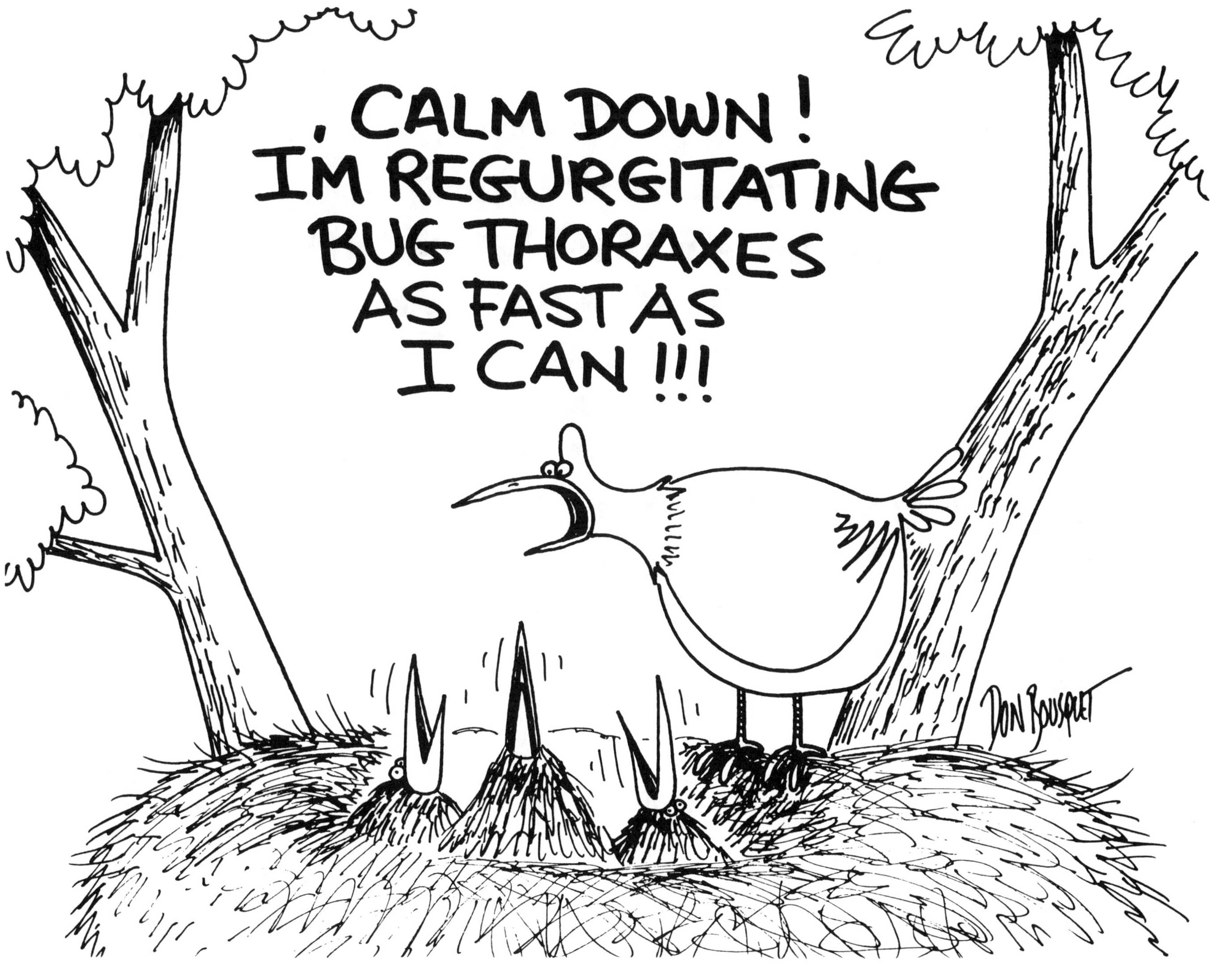
CALM DOWN! I'M REGURGITATING BUG THORAXES AS FAST AS I CAN!!!
DON BOUSQUET

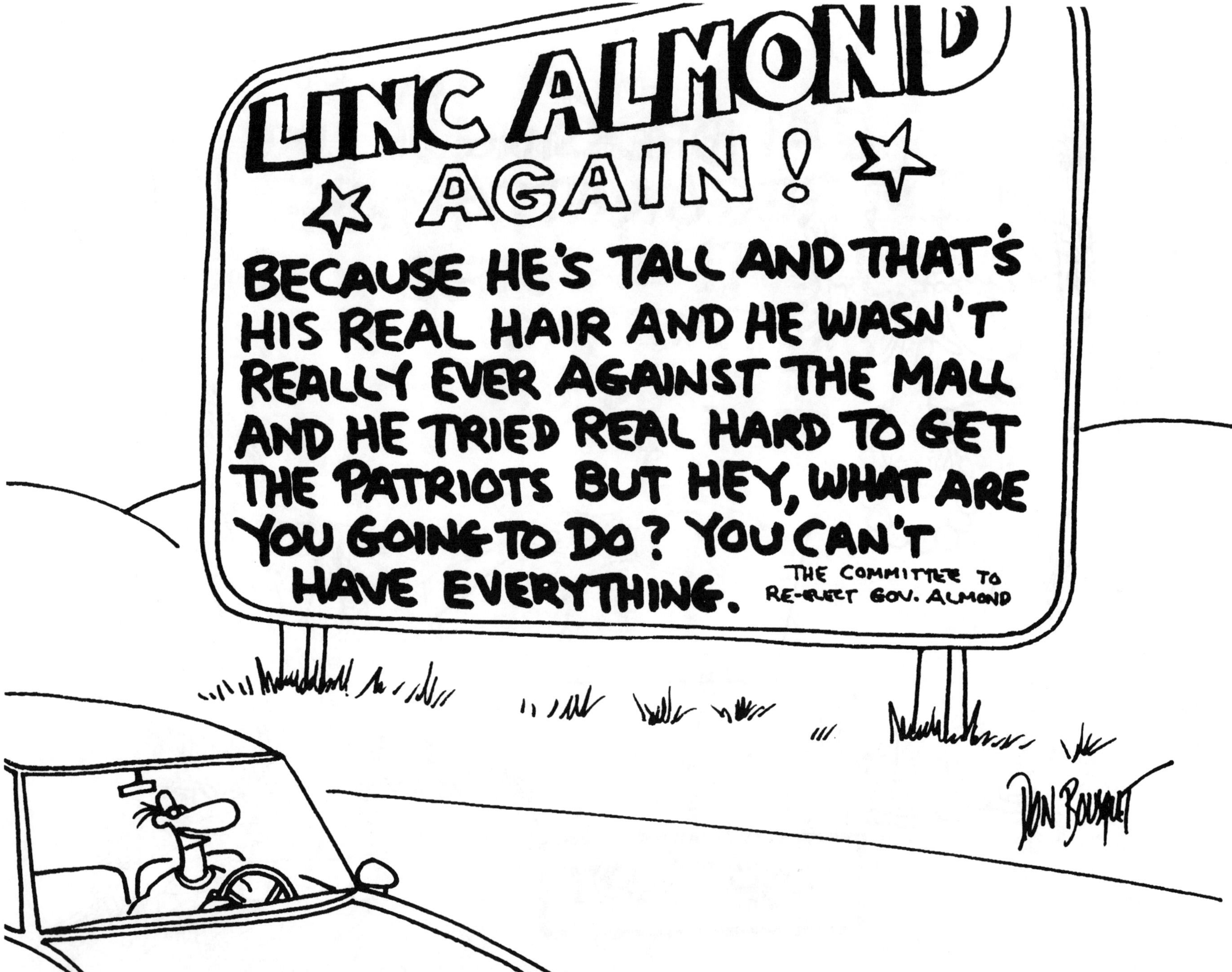
LINC ALMOND
AGAIN!
BECAUSE HE'S TALL AND THAT'S HIS REAL HAIR AND HE WASN'T REALLY EVER AGAINST THE MALL AND HE TRIED REAL HARD TO GET THE PATRIOTS BUT HEY, WHAT ARE YOU GOING TO DO? YOU CAN'T HAVE EVERYTHING.
THE COMMITTEE TO RE-ELECT GOV. ALMOND
DON BOUSQUET

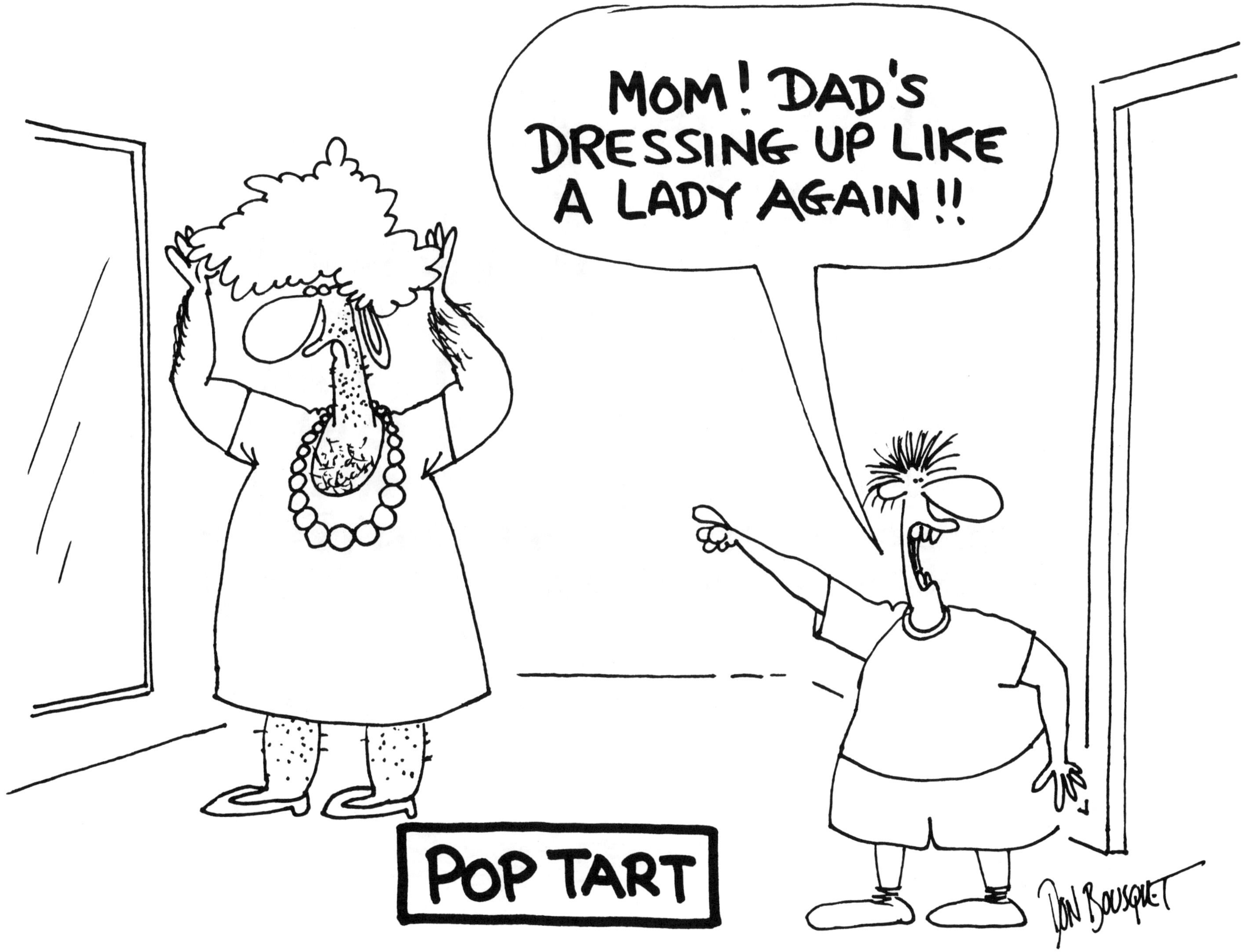
MOM! DAD'S DRESSING UP LIKE A LADY AGAIN!!
POP TART
DON BOUSQUET

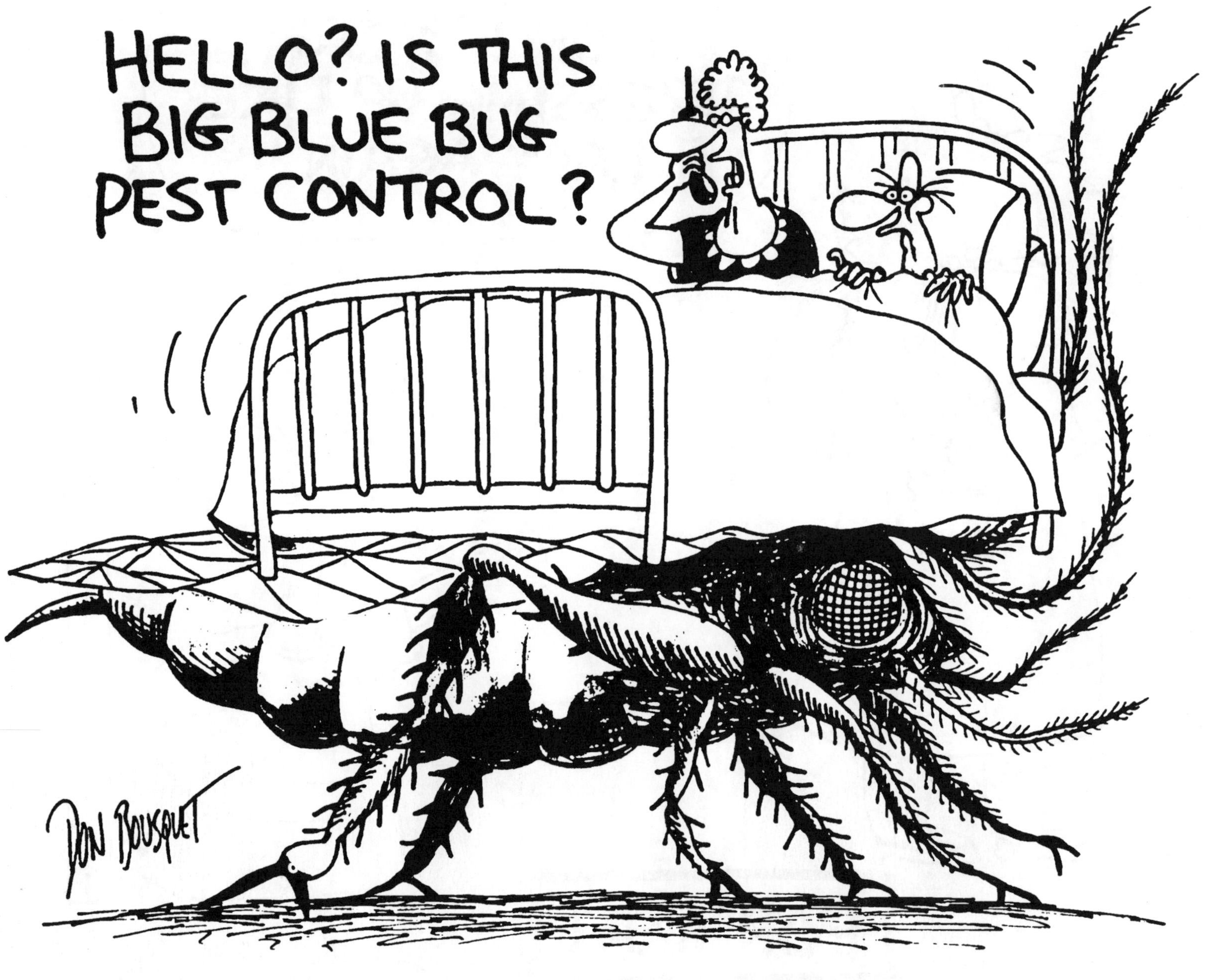
HELLO? IS THIS BIG BLUE BUG PEST CONTROL?
DON BOUSQUET